Praise for *Why Can't I Have Everything?* . . .

Kids will love the fun literature and engaging activities in *Why Can't I Have Everything?* Teachers will welcome the easy-to-use format and in-depth curriculum, and parents will appreciate the valuable lessons their children learn from this book.

—Trudy Harris, elementary school teacher, Idaho Falls, Idaho,
and author of *Jenny Found a Penny* and *100 Days of School*

Why Can't I Have Everything? is so timely. Children are becoming more and more aware of the importance of money in their world. As a mother of a two preschoolers and as a math specialist, I highly recommend this thoughtful collection of lessons, children's literature suggestions, and assessments. The teaching tips and key questions, along with the friendly format, make this the perfect resource for those trying to answer the question, "Why Can't I Have Everything?" The lessons will engage future consumers at home and at school. Jane's knowledge of young mathematicians has resulted in another book that is right on the money.

—Beth Terry, math specialist,
Alexandria City Public Schools, Virginia,
and 2004 PAEMST Awardee–Colorado

Jane Crawford has created a practical and timely resource that prepares young children to be financially literate and responsible consumers. *Why I Can't Have Everything?* is full of engaging, standards-based lessons that integrate math, social studies, and language arts. Teachers and parents will love this book.

—Rusty Bresser, lecturer and supervisor of teacher education,
University of California, San Diego, and coauthor of
Supporting English Language Learners in Math Class

Why Can't I Have Everything? is a rich resource for teachers and parents alike. Thoughtful selections of outstanding children's literature enhance increasingly complex mathematical lessons. Young children begin with coin recognition and counting. Lessons then evolve to consider large numbers and place value patterns. Each chapter is loaded with meaningful real-life connections that coax children beyond their immediate egocentric perspectives to consider how money affects others in their communities and their world. Key questions and teacher notes clarify ways that adults can help children build vocabulary and deepen understanding. This resource provides a wonderful context for helping young mathematical thinkers develop number sense in meaningful ways.

—Vicki Bachman, math consultant,
Grant Wood Area Education Agency,
Cedar Rapids, Iowa

Grades PreK-2

Why Can't I Have EVERYTHING?

Teaching Today's Children to Be
Financially and Mathematically Savvy

Jane Crawford

Foreword by Marilyn Burns

Math Solutions

Sausalito, California, USA

Math Solutions
One Harbor Drive, Suite 101
Sausalito, California, USA 94965
www.mathsolutions.com

Library of Congress Cataloging-in-Publication Data
Crawford, Jane.
    Why can't I have everything? : teaching today's children to be financially and
    mathematically savvy : grades prek–2 / Jane Crawford.
       p. cm.
    ISBN 978-1-935099-25-3
    1. Financial literacy—Juvenile literature. 2. Money—Juvenile literature.
    3. Consumption (Economics)—Juvenile literature. I. Title.
    HG173.8.C73 2012
    372.82—dc22   2011004847

Editor: Jamie Ann Cross
Production service: Element LLC
Production coordinator: Melissa L. Inglis-Elliott
Cover design: Wanda Espana/Wee Design
Cover image: "Girl putting a penny into a glass piggy bank" © Geri Lavrov/
    Photographer's Choice/Getty Images
Interior design: Element LLC
Interior images: "Fist full of change" © Jodi Kelly/iStockphoto.com.
    Dana Islas's class at Pueblo Gardens Elementary School, Tucson, Arizona. Videographer:
    Friday's Films, www.fridaysfilms.com
Composition: Element LLC

11 10 9 8 7 6 5 4 3 2   31   22 21 20 19 18 17 16 15 14 13

A Message from Math Solutions

We at Math Solutions believe that teaching math well calls for increasing our understanding of the math we teach, seeking deeper insights into how students learn mathematics, and refining our lessons to best promote students' learning.

Math Solutions shares classroom-tested lessons and teaching expertise from our faculty of professional development consultants as well as from other respected math educators. Our publications are part of the nationwide effort we've made since 1984 that now includes

- more than five hundred face-to-face professional development programs each year for teachers and administrators in districts across the country;
- professional development books that span all math topics taught in kindergarten through high school;
- videos for teachers and for parents that show math lessons taught in actual classrooms;
- on-site visits to schools to help refine teaching strategies and assess student learning; and
- free online support, including grade-level lessons, book reviews, inservice information, and district feedback, all in our Math Solutions Online Newsletter.

For information about all of the products and services we have available, please visit our website at *www.mathsolutions.com.* You can also contact us to discuss math professional development needs by calling (800) 868-9092 or by sending an email to *info@mathsolutions.com.*

We're always eager for your feedback and interested in learning about your particular needs. We look forward to hearing from you.

To the teachers and parents who believe in the importance of children having both mathematical and financial knowledge.

Brief Contents

Contents

Reproducibles

Foreword

In 1996 Jane Crawford wrote a book for our Math By All Means series titled *Money: Grades 1–2*. It was truly a privilege for me to work with Jane when she was writing that book. I learned a great deal and the teaching ideas in that resource have served me well in my work with young students. In the Preface, I wrote, "I came to understand what makes Jane a master teacher and why she received the 1993 Presidential Award for Excellence in Teaching Mathematics."

When I learned that Jane was writing a new teacher resource about money, I was curious to learn what new perspectives Jane brought to the subject. And I was intrigued by the title—*Why Can't I Have Everything*?

After reading the book, I was thrilled. This new book by Jane models all that is important about effective math teaching for young children. The book addresses questions that are important to all children's lives: What is money? Why do we need money? How do we get money? What are the differences between wanting and needing? What about saving and sharing? It presents lessons that engage students with these important ideas through hands-on activities that also give experience with counting, estimating, place value, adding and subtracting, data, and solving word problems. The teaching directions are clear, the sidebar insights are helpful and supportive, and Jane's connection to classroom teaching is evident. Also included are specific suggestions for connecting with parents.

And along with the focus on money and mathematics, the book is rich with references to language arts. Children's literature is integrated throughout. Students ponder figures of speech about money: saving for a rainy day, what are nest eggs, what does it mean to say that money doesn't grow on trees, and more. They explore the many meanings of *change*—change a light bulb, change your mind, change clothing, change in your pocket, getting change from a dollar, and more. They learn the many ways we use the word *bank*—the bank of a river, how airplanes bank, when we bank on a person to do her job, and, of course, a bank as a safe place to put money. They learn the history about who appears on our money, about credit cards, debit cards, gift cards, and also about capital, revenue, earnings, goods, services, interest, loans, and microfinancing.

The book presents hard issues: how sometimes having everything means being left with nothing, about earning money beyond tooth fairies and allowances, what are the consequences and rewards of borrowing, and why we have to pay back more when we borrow money. The teaching suggestions in the book make these difficult and often complex issues accessible to children.

Why Can't I Have Everything? promises to provide teachers and parents ways to help children become mathematically and financially savvy. And it delivers on this promise. This book is truly a treasure. With this book, Jane has brought being a master teacher to a new level.

—MARILYN BURNS
FOUNDER, MATH SOLUTIONS

Acknowledgments

Marilyn Burns's commitment to children and mathematics has always been an inspiration to me. I want to convey my appreciation for opportunities and challenges she has given to me over the years.

A special thanks also goes to Beth Terry for reading every word written and offering feedback. Her expertise, insights, and friendship are important to me.

I also want to thank Jamie Cross for her encouragement, patience, and thoughtful attention to the details in this book. Without her this book wouldn't have happened.

Lastly, thanks goes to Lindsay Crawford, my husband, for persevering through this project.

—JANE CRAWFORD

Why This Resource and How to Use It

Right now the world is trying to emerge from a terrible recession. It has been predicted that the generation growing up in this recession will earn less money than their parents but will save more. Economists and educators are suggesting that economic ideas are important enough to teach at all levels. People who never considered teaching or taking business classes are thinking about economics, both their personal finances and the finances of our nation and the world. Teachers are being asked to teach economics to young children when traditionally it was taught only to high school or college students.

Why Can't I Have Everything? Teaching Today's Children to Be Financially and Mathematically Savvy is an important, timely resource containing in-depth support for teachers in integrating money and economics ideas into their teaching. This resource offers more than forty lessons categorized by seven important financial literacy themes for young learners. The lessons build on one another within each chapter. The lessons include literature connections, corresponding formative assessments, games, suggestions for differentiating instruction, ideas for parents, and alignments to the Common Core State Standards in Mathematics. In the appendices you'll find reproducible letters for parents to go with the lessons, plus a final project that ties together all the lessons.

Though there is an abundance of financial literacy material on the market, very little conveys an understanding of child development or good teaching. In fact, many of these resources are funded by banking institutions whose aim is to have children grow up, save money, and deposit it in their institution. Of the material available, there is even less that targets the preK–2 grade span, even though research indicates that students can learn economic concepts in the primary grades.

Students not only need to develop a good sense of numbers but also need to become literate about money issues. These lessons provide opportunities to ask questions—questions that give students reasons to think about bigger ideas associated with earning and spending money. These lessons also provide students with opportunities to identify, count, and use money in a problem-solving or game situation.

Children need to talk about saving for something special versus saving for a rainy day. Students should be able to describe the difference between those things we want and those things we need. They also need to bump into the idea of consequences when we don't manage money well.

Financial Fact

In 2008 President George W. Bush signed an Executive Order creating a President's Advisory Council on Financial Literacy. That council, in its first report to the president, recommended improving financial literacy among children of all ages, from preschool through postsecondary education.

This resource offers more than forty lessons categorized by seven important financial literacy themes for young learners. The lessons build on one another within each chapter.

Though there is an abundance of financial literacy material on the market, very little conveys an understanding of child development or good teaching.

But I Don't Have Time to Teach Financial Literacy . . .

In our busy schedules, the last thing needed is one more unit to teach. Per research done by Networks Financial Institute, elementary teachers who do not teach financial literacy primarily do so because of time constraints and the fact that they are not comfortable teaching it. *Why Can't I Have Everything? Teaching Today's Children to Be Financially and Mathematically Savvy* offers timesaving, classroom-tested lessons. The lessons are not "one more unit"—rather they are carefully integrated with familiar content areas—mathematics, writing, reading, and economics; provide ample teaching support; and target almost every state's economic standards, as well as the Common Core State Standards for Mathematics. Per one reader's comments, "Integrating financial literacy in subjects already taught, i.e., math, writing, social studies, rather than making it a separate topic will be welcomed by teachers who already have to teach too much in a too short a time frame."

How Do These Lessons Fit in My Curriculum?

All of the lessons in this book have connections to economics standards (see the Economics Objectives in the Appendix) and/or the Common Core State Standards for Mathematics. You may find some lessons with only economics standards. Other lessons may have only mathematical objectives. Most lessons have both economic and mathematical connections. All of these lessons are important if we want to ensure that children are mathematically and financially savvy—the two go together.

 All of the lessons in this book have connections to economics standards (see the Economics Objectives in the Appendix) and/or the Common Core State Standards for Mathematics.

How Are These Lessons Connected to PreK–2 Math?

Developing Number Sense and Counting Skills

In these lessons, students write, count money, communicate, and develop number sense in addition to being introduced to economic ideas. The lessons target students by the development of number concepts rather than grade level. Until students are able to count by ones, fives, and tens, counting money is difficult.

 In these lessons, students write, count money, communicate, and develop number sense in addition to being introduced to economic ideas.

The counting process begins with children before they start the formal education process. Preschoolers may count objects or rote count but may not always have the numbers in the correct order. These preschoolers are aware of numbers and are in the process of becoming ready for formal counting instruction. They are ready to be exposed to the concept of money and should have supervised opportunities to handle coins and watch parents and caregivers use money.

A Note About the Economics Goals for Lessons in This Resource

The National Council of Economics Educators, in a survey published in March 2005, found that forty-nine states plus the District of Columbia include economics in their standards. There are no national benchmarks for students below grade 4. State by state, these standards are somewhat similar but differ in the form they take and sometimes the content.

Voluntary National Content Standards in Economics were published by the Council of Economics Education in 1997 and have recently been revised and updated. The revised standards, published in 2010, contain twenty economics content standards. These are benchmarked at grades 4, 8, and 12. These standards are concerned with economic concepts rather than just facts. They present an outline for students to encounter the most important and enduring knowledge, ideas, and issues in economics. These standards can be found at www.councilforeconed.org/ea/standards/pdf.

States are in the process of developing their own versions of economic standards and testing requirements at different grade levels. Some states follow the voluntary standards in benchmarking at grades 4, 8, and 12. Other states developed specific requirements at every grade level. Most states include the same economic ideas and objectives but publish their standards in a variety of formats.

I compiled economic ideas and objectives from most of the states having benchmarks for every grade. I wrote them as economic objectives (see the Appendix). Teachers using this book should be aware that these objectives may or may not match their state standards. When their own state standards differ from these objectives, teachers should always follow their state requirements.

Children in prekindergarten and early kindergarten have opportunities to rote count and begin putting numbers in the correct order. They are developing readiness for future, more sophisticated counting. Kindergarten students (and some early first graders) often count to a number that is less than twenty early in the school year. Some students rote count to one hundred or more but fail to show one-to-one correspondence when they count objects. Often these early rote counters fail to tag objects with the number name as they count. These young students don't always display one-to-one correspondence and fail to keep track of what they have counted and what is left to count. Some of these students do not realize the last number they say is the quantity of things they are counting. These students are ready to learn to identify and start counting pennies. Counting by ones is something these children enjoy doing. Other coins should also be introduced to these early counters. These students also have a very short range in terms of acquiring time concepts. Asking these students to plan their economic future would not be developmentally appropriate.

Rational counters are students who display confidence in counting; they use one-to-one correspondence when counting a group of objects. They are able to rote count to one hundred or more. They tag objects with a number word as they count. They realize that the last object counted is the quantity of objects in the group. These students are developing the ability to count by ones, twos, fives, and tens. They are ready to count money! These students have an expanded knowledge of time. They are beginning to learn about calendars and can look forward to holidays, celebrations, and vacations. Asking them to think of saving money for something they want or need in the near future is appropriate.

Why Is Each Lesson Connected to Literature?

These lessons are all connected to literature. The literature is used to open financial discussions with your students. Financial literacy topics are very sophisticated for young learners. Literature provides a way to connect with students' prior knowledge and present new ideas. The books and financial discussions can be used in one setting and the math lessons in another, or in combination.

Financial literacy topics are very sophisticated for young learners. Literature provides a way to connect with students' prior knowledge and present new ideas.

Each chapter references more than one picture book. Many of these books are classics that you may find in your libraries. Some of these books may go in and out of print over the years. Some books, such as the award-winning title *A Chair for My Mother*, by Vera Williams, are beautiful children's literature that you would share with students even without connecting to financial literacy. Other books listed in lessons are very topic-specific and do a good job of relaying information. These books are less likely to be standard read-aloud literature.

What Materials Do These Lessons Require?

The Use of Money

The use of real money is the best in all lessons. Plastic money is available and suggested by many books about children and money on the market today. In some situations there would be no difference in the lesson with real or fake money.

The use of real money is the best in all lessons.

In identifying coins, the use of real coins is important. I suggest parents provide ten dimes, twenty nickels, and fifty pennies for their student. In my own classroom I always request money from parents, saying that money will be used in the classroom for money-counting lessons. If parents send a written request, coins are returned at the end of the year. If I don't get a letter from parents, I assume the $2.50 is a donation to use in money counting, and to possibly purchase an end-of-year snack for students. Usually parents expect the coins to be a donation. A sample letter to parents is included (see the Appendix) for your assistance in writing that letter.

The Use of Socks

Early in the school year I always keep a list of donation items I hope parents can contribute for classroom use. Socks are always on that list. I tell parents we don't need matched stocks. Using socks instead of paper or cloth bags keeps children from peaking inside to choose a specific coin. My classroom supply of socks is always plentiful. Another item to ask for is small plastic containers if you don't already have a supply.

What Is My Role as the Teacher in These Lessons?

It is your role as the teacher to present information about money and economic ideas in an interesting and positive way and to give students opportunities to work with and talk to other students. Some lessons are designed as whole-group lessons, involving each student in the same activity. Reading literature aloud is usually a whole-group activity. Other lessons will work best in small groups or pairs of students. For all lessons, the teacher is a facilitator rather than a lecturer.

For all lessons, the teacher is a facilitator rather than a lecturer.

How Do I Assess Students When Using These Lessons?

Every chapter in this resource concludes with a formative assessment section to give you ideas and support in assessing students when using these lessons. Economic ideas presented to young children are not always easy to assess. Some of the ideas are given at an introductory level and do not require assessment in the kindergarten or first-grade classrooms. Other assessments, such as money-counting skills, can best be accomplished with quick one-on-one assessments. The results of these assessments may tell you that students need more class time spent on certain skills or that students are proficient and it is time to move on to other skills.

Every chapter in this resource concludes with a formative assessment section to give you ideas and support in assessing students when using these lessons.

Can Parents Use These Lessons?

Parents can definitely use these lessons—though the lesson directions are in the context of the classroom, they can easily be adapted for use at home and/or in home schooling contexts! Each lesson includes an "Ideas for Parents" section to facilitate such adaptations, plus each chapter offers a "Letter for the Parents" that the teachers can use to make school–home connections. In addition, each chapter of this book concludes with an Additional Ideas for Parents section,

Each chapter concludes with an Additional Ideas for Parents section, suggesting additional ways for parents to informally assess their child and further practice the financial and mathematical ideas with their children.

suggesting additional ways for parents to informally assess their child and further practice the financial and mathematical ideas with their children. Some suggestions may allow parents to take their natural conversations with children about money to a higher level. The literature used in each chapter provides good stories that lead to conversations about money at school and at home. Most of these books are readily available, very popular, and likely to stay in print. The games parts of some lessons are also appropriate to use at home; games are an enjoyable way for parents to reinforce the financial and mathematical knowledge that their child is acquiring.

There are more opportunities, in real-life context, at home to learn about money than at school. Children develop ideas about money from home. They watch our habits, overhear us talk about money and spending, and begin to form their own ideas about money. At school children often learn coin recognition and values, whereas at home children learn the importance of money in their own lives. At school children participate in simulations of shopping experiences, whereas at home children often shop with their parents. At school children are generally given a specific definition or explanation of money-related ideas. At home children develop ideas based on observation. It is very easy for children to assume that a credit card or checkbook provides unlimited funds unless parents talk with children and help them develop an understanding about money, its various forms, and what limits come with each.

> There are more opportunities, in real-life context, at home to learn about money than at school. Children develop ideas about money from home.

Common Core State Standards for Mathematics Correlations

All lessons are correlated to the Common Core State Standards when applicable. The correlations are listed with grade (K, 1, or 2) first, followed by the abbreviated domain, followed by the exact strand number(s).

Lesson/Title	Counting and Cardinality (CC)	Operations and Algebraic Thinking (OA)	Number and Operations in Base Ten (NBT)	Measurement and Data (MD)
Common Core State Standards for Mathematics Domain				
1.4 A Penny a Day	K.CC.1.4.5		1.NBT.1.2.a.b.c 2.NBT.2	2.MD.8
1.5 A Number a Day		1.OA.1.5 2.OA.1.2	K.NBT.1 2.NBT.2.5.8	2.MD.8
1.6 Race to a Quarter		1.OA.7	1.NBT.1.2.a 2.NBT.2	2.MD.8
2.1 The Trouble with Money				K.MD.3 1.MD.4 2.MD.10
2.3 Do You Get an Allowance?				K.MD.3 1.MD.4 2.MD.10
2.4 Introducing the Counting Jar	K.CC.1.2.3.4.a.b.c.5		1.NBT.1.2.a 2.NBT.2	2.MD.8
2.5 How Much Money Is in the Counting Jar?		2.OA.4	1.NBT.1.2.a 2.NBT.2	2.MD.8
2.6 Counting Jars for Small Groups	K.CC.1.2.3.4.a.b.c.5		1.NBT.1.2.a	
2.7 How Much Money Did the Tooth Fairy Leave?				K.MD.3 1.MD.4 2.MD.10
2.8 Counting Combinations of Pennies and Dimes			1.NBT.1.2.a.b.c 2.NBT.2.8	2.MD.8
3.1 What's a Half-Dollar?			1.NBT.1.2.a.b.c 2.NBT.1.a.b.2.7	2.MD.8
3.2 Jenny Found a Penny			1.NBT.2.4 2.NBT.1.a.2.5	K.MD.3 1.MD.4 2.MD.8.10
3.3 A Penny Hunt	K.CC.1.2.4.a.b.c.5	1.OA.7		1.MD.4
3.4 A Quarter from the Tooth Fairy		1.OA.1.2.3.7 2.OA.1	2.NBT.2	2.MD.8
3.5 Being "Smart" About Trading Money		1.OA.1	2.NBT.2	2.MD.8
3.6 Getting Change Back	K.CC.1.2.4.5	1.OA.1.2.4.5.6.7.8 2.OA.1	1.NBT.2.a.b.c.3.4.5.6 2.NBT.1.a.2.5.6.8	2.MD.8
4.3 Alexander Used to Be Rich		1.OA.1 2.OA.1	2.NBT.2	2.MD.8
4.4 May I Have Tomatoes for Cilantro?	K.CC.4.a.b.c.5	1.OA.5.6		1.MD.4 2.MD.10

(Continued)

Lesson/Title	Counting and Cardinality (CC)	Operations and Algebraic Thinking (OA)	Number and Operations in Base Ten (NBT)	Measurement and Data (MD)
4.5 What Will We Find in the Store Today?	K.CC.4.a.b.c.5	1.OA.5.6		1.MD.4 2.MD.10
4.6 The Grab and Go! Game	K.CC.6		1.NBT.2.a.b.c.3 2.NBT.4	2.MD.8
5.1 Arthur's Funny Money			1.NBT.2.a.b.c 2.NBT.1.a.b.2.7	2.MD.8
5.2 Have You Ever Been Paid for Doing Something?				1.MD.4 2.MD.10
5.3 Goods and Services				1.MD.4 2.MD.10
5.4 Ox-Cart Man	K.CC.5			
5.5 My Rows and Piles of Money	K.CC.1.4.a.b.c.5.7	2.OA.4	1.NBT.1.2.a.b.c 2.NBT.1.a.b.2.3	2.MD.8
5.6 Pennies for Elephants			1.NBT.2.a.c.4 2.NBT.1.a.7	
5.7 Connecting Money to the Properties of Addition		K.OA.1 1.OA.3.4.5.6.7.8	2.NBT.5.6.7.9	
6.1 A Chair for My Mother	K.CC.6.7	1.OA.1.7 2.OA.1.3		1.MD.4 2.MD.8
6.2 A Hat for Miss Eula	K.CC.5.6.7			K.MD.3 1.MD.4 2.MD.10
6.3 Benny's Pennies	K.CC.2.3.4.a.b.c.5.6	K.OA.2.3 1.OA.1.6.7.8		
6.4 How Much Money Do I Have Now? Game			1.NBT.2.a.b.c.4 2.NBT.1.a.8	
6.5 Using Quarters for Landmarks		2.OA.1	1.NBT.1.2.4.5 2.NBT.2.5.8.9	
6.6 Acting Out Money-Sharing Problems	K.CC.5	K.OA.1.2.3.4.5		
7.1 What Is a Bank?		1.OA.5 2.OA.1	1.NBT.1	2.MD.8
7.2 How Many Coins Are in That Stack?	K.CC.5		2.NBT.2	2.MD.8
7.3 What Is Interest?		1.OA.5 2.OA.1	1.NBT.1	2.MD.8
7.4 What Is a Loan?		1.OA.5 2.OA.1	1.NBT.1	2.MD.8
7.5 How One Small Loan Made a Big Difference	K.CC.1	2.OA.1	2.NBT.2 2.NBT.8	2.MD.8
7.6 Should I Use a Credit Card?		1.OA.5 2.OA.1	1.NBT.1	2.MD.8
7.7 Using Debit and Gift Cards	K.NBT.3			1.MD.4 2.MD.10

Why Can't I Have EVERYTHING?

Teaching Today's Children to Be Financially and Mathematically Savvy

Jane Crawford

Foreword by Marilyn Burns

Math Solutions
Sausalito, California, USA

CHAPTER 1

What Is Money?

Introduce the History of Money, Coins, and Coin Values

Overview

A first step in helping children be financially and mathematically savvy is to build their understanding of what exactly is money. From identifying and handling money to learning the history of it, the explorations in these lessons get students thinking, drawing, writing, and talking about those shiny coins in their parents' pockets.

Lesson 1.1 features children's voices responding to and exploring key questions such as "Why do we need money?" and "How do we get money?" (The idea of bartering is introduced and will be revisited in Chapter 4.)

Lessons 1.2 and **1.3** give students a unique opportunity (magnifying glass in hand!) to learn more about what's on a coin.

Mathematically, students are asked to count money starting with **Lesson 1.4**, *A Penny a Day*.

In **Lessons 1.4** through **1.6** students have opportunities to identify and count coins, trade coins, and find equivalent collections of coins. A wide array of literature—from Cat in the Hat's *One Cent, Two Cents, Old Cent, New Cent* to *Money Madness*—provides factual information about money and coins in visually engaging, entertaining formats.

The Lessons

Formative Assessment
23

Formative Assessment Checklist
24

Literature Used in This Chapter

One Cent, Two Cents, Old Cent, New Cent by Bonnie Worth

The Story of Money by Betsy Maestro

Welcome Books: Money Matters series *(Dimes, Dollars, Nickels, Pennies, Quarters)* by Mary Hill

The Coin Counting Book by Rozanne Lanczak Williams

Money Madness by David A. Adler

Smart About Money by Jon Lee Anderson

Additional Idea$ for Parent$

What Is Money?

An economics lesson for young learners

Overview

I'm the Cat in the Hat

and you know something funny?

We're about to have fun

learning all about money!

—*One Cent, Two Cents, Old Cent, New Cent*

In this lesson students first think about and discuss answers to the key questions, "What is money? Why do we need money? How do we get money?" After lively discussion, students launch into the study of money and its history, from the ancient practice of bartering to minting coins to banking. Students read the popular Cat in the Hat book, *One Cent, Two Cents, Old Cent, New Cent* (alternatively, second graders may read *The Story of Money*)—both visually engaging and entertaining introductions to the world of money. Extensions offer additional reading selections—whether it be imagining a world without money in *Money Madness* or learning how Bill turns a class assignment into a monetary venture in *Smart About Money*.

Economics Goals

Students will show:
▶ understanding of the Concept of Money by:
  • recognizing various forms of U.S. currency
▶ understanding of the Concept of Goods and Services by:
  • explaining the difference in purchasing and bartering for goods and services

Materials

paper for drawing and writing

pencils

Time

1 class period

Literature Connections

• *One Cent, Two Cents, Old Cent, New Cent* by Bonnie Worth
• *The Story of Money* by Betsy Maestro
• *Smart About Money* by Jon Lee Anderson
• *Money Madness* by David A. Adler

Teaching Directions

Part 1: Introducing the Lesson

1. Gather students in the whole-group area of your classroom. Before you start reading, ask the key question, "What is money?" Give students time to think and then share what they know about money.

2. After students have finished telling what they think money is, ask them, "Why do we need money?" Again, give students time to tell what they think about our needs for money.

3. Finally, explain that you are going to ask one more question but you want students to respond in writing. Give each student paper. When students understand the assignment, ask them the question: "How do we get money?"

4. When students have completed writing and drawing, ask them to share their work in a whole-group setting. Ask nonwriters to explain their drawings. Make notes on the back of drawings to explain what each child said. See the following examples of student responses.

Part 2: Reading the Book

5. After the above money discussion, read the popular Cat in the Hat children's book, *One Cent, Two Cents, Old Cent, New Cent* aloud to your class. Second-grade teachers might want to use Betsy Maestro's *The Story of Money*. Both children's picture books give a fascinating introduction to the study of money and its history, beginning with the ancient practice of bartering.

6. As you are reading, allow time for students to respond to illustrations or information given. Pause after reading about bartering. Ask students if they have ever traded lunch or snacks with another student. Allow a few students to talk about trading. Explain that bartering is trading. Help students make connections between bartering and the invention of money.

Key Questions

What is money?

Why do we need money?

How do we get money?

Teaching Insight: Differentiating the Writing Task

If your students are at an age to write, then ask them to write the answer to the question. If your students are prewriters, ask them to draw a picture to show the answer. First graders may be able to draw a picture and write a little to explain their drawings.

Teaching Insight: Students' Responses

Collect and sort students' papers so you will know how many students believe money grows on trees or is unlimited from parents and how many know money is paid for goods or services. It may be interesting to notice where students' money comes from. You might have responses such as tooth fairies and grandmas. Some students might indicate that they get allowances.

Teaching Insight: Picture Books

When reading picture books in whole-group settings, consider using a document camera or some form of technology that will project the illustrations for the whole class to more easily see.

Children's Voices

Following are samples of students' responses to the key questions in Part 1 of this lesson.

PreKindergarten

Children's verbal explanations of their answers to the questions.

What is money?
- It's cash. It's gray.
- One cent. It looks like a circle.
- Money is like quarters and pennies.

Why do we need money?
- You can buy stuff for your house . . . food, grapes, bread, corn, macaroni, greens, juice if you don't have any for your house, snacks like chips and licorice.
- We need to buy something like toys, cars, computers, clothes, TVs, and some toy animals.
- To buy something.
- When you are hungry, you have to get something to eat.

How do we get money?
- You get money from the bank—put it in and they give you more out.
- You get it from people that sell money. People that put presidents on a coin.
- To ask your auntie or your mommy.
- You get cash from car insurance.

Kindergarten

Children's verbal explanations of their answers to the questions.

What is money?
- Money, you pay for something.
- You buy something.
- This is a money tree. You get money and get rich. *(This student drew a money tree.)*
- Dollars is money.
- It's change that you buy something with.
- Something you spend.
- Money is quarters, pennies, dimes, and cents.
- Money is a kind of thing you use to pay for something. It could be a circle or a rectangle.
- Money is something you spend on food you want. It's green. I think Abraham Lincoln is on it and it's worth one cent.
- It's like change and dollars.
- It's green.
- It kind of looks like green paper and it's a dollar. Coins look like hard circles and they're little.
- Money is something you can buy stuff with. Some money is a circle and some are rectangles.

Why do we need money?
- If you don't have money, you will be hungry.
- You buy stuff like cookies and stereos.
- You buy food with it.
- To buy stuff.
- Because it's for people, like people in Haiti.

- You get to buy stuff.
- Because you need to get more and more. But don't go to a stranger to get money.
- You can buy food and clothes and be healthy.
- So we can buy food and water and stuff. You can buy fridges and stuff.
- So you can buy stuff. I had something like a video game with money.
- To buy stuff like a car and medicine.
- We need it to buy things we need.
- We need it to buy food and things we need.
- Pay for stuff and food.

How do we get money?
- You can get cash and have money.
- You get a job and that's how you get money.
- Go to your "cash" all the time and get more.
- Look in your purse to see if you have it or ask somebody like my dad.
- Making money when you are doing a job.
- From people. They make money. My mom makes money-she uses circles and puts people on it.
- At the store. If you buy food at the store, the man or lady will give you money.

- We get it by working.
- You can get it from a bank . . . or by working.
- You get it from having a job.
- Get it by working.
- You have to save up to buy something that is really high.
- You need a job to get money or you can find it on the ground sometimes.
- If you find money on the floor, somebody will take it even if they don't know who it is.
- Go to the bank and tell them, "where is the money machine at?"

First Grade

Children's written explanations of their answers to the questions.

What is money?

Why do we need money?

How do we get money?
- Mune is sube. You git muny. You mak mue. You biy suf wif mue.
- Moundey is cash.
- Money is cash and to bie thes.
- Money is that you spid it and quarters and dimes.

- Money is sumthing that you save.
- Mne is wen you biey soda like ice cream yro ata dbar.
- Mney is samtheing that you save for good thaings.
- Mony is suthing that you big suff with like toys and needs and this how you get mony you have to woke for mony.

- Money is something that peple can spend at a store the color is green.
- Muney is like wan you go to the stowr and you biey.
- Money is something that you pay with money is inpodet. You pay your credit card bill. I love money.
- Muney is thufing that you big thaz.

Extensions

Read *Money Madness* by David A. Adler, in which the reader first imagines a world without money then navigates the history of money through bright, engaging artwork and storytelling. Have a class discussion about the difficulties parents would encounter if they had to barter for everything instead of using money.

If you are teaching second grade, the book *Smart About Money: A Rich History* by Jon Lee Anderson is a good addition to your classroom reading library. In this book, Ms. Brandt asks her class to write a report on a subject of interest to each of her students. Bill chooses the subject of money, and the story takes off from there. In addition to being an entertaining look at the history of money, this book provides an example of report writing.

Idea$ for Parent$

Give children many opportunities to think about what money is, why we need money, and how we get money. Read the books in this lesson at home with your child. Encourage discussions on money and its history. When you ask the three questions listed in Lesson 1.1 ("*What is money? Why do we need money? How do we get money?*"), you may gain insight into your child's ideas about money from the answers you receive. Consider explaining where your household money comes from using general terms. For example, "I have to go to work to get the money we spend when we go to the store." Your child's responses may indicate that your child believes the checkbook is unlimited. Without revealing the details of your financial situation, involve your child in your bill-paying and bank-depositing processes.

For further insights on helping your child with coin recognition, see the section, Additional Ideas for Parents, page 25. See also the Letter to the Parents, page 231.

Beginning to Identify Coins
Coin identification practice for young learners

Overview

Children need to identify coins before they can learn coin values. In this lesson, students explore what's on a penny by first doing a coin rubbing, then working in partners and a whole-group setting to discuss the penny's characteristics. Mary Hill's Welcome Books: Money Matters series (*Pennies, Nickels, Dimes, Quarters*) provides an engaging literary extension.

Economics Goals

Students will show:
▶ understanding of the Concept of Money by:
  • recognizing various forms of U.S. currency
  • recognizing that different countries have different coins

Materials

penny, 1 per student

magnifier, 1 per student or pair of students

pencil or crayon to make rubbings, 1 per student

newsprint or plain white paper, 1 sheet per student

chart paper

Time

1 class period

Literature Connections

Welcome Books: Money Matters series (*Pennies, Nickels, Dimes, Quarters*) by Mary Hill

Teaching Directions

Part 1: Rubbing Pennies

1. Give each child a penny and a piece of paper. Explain that they will be doing coin rubbings. Demonstrate before having students create rubbings by holding the paper tight over the coin and rubbing a pencil lead or crayon gently over the surface until the image on the coin appears on the paper.

2. Have students do their own rubbings. When they are done, they should write the word *penny* by their rubbing.

Part 2: Inspecting Pennies

3. Starting the lesson with a rubbing of the coin help students focus on the face of the coin and creates interest in exploring what is on the coin. Now tell students you want them to work with their partner to find all the important things about pennies.

4. When students have had a minute or two to look closely at their pennies with a partner, gather them as a whole group. Ask students, "What did you find on your penny?" Make a list of things that students find on their pennies (use chart paper or some means of displaying the list for everyone to see).

5. If you have a classroom set of magnifiers, allow students to use them to inspect their coins. Expect students to find *In God We Trust*, *Liberty*, a date, and Lincoln's picture on the front of a penny. On the back students should find *one cent* and the Lincoln Memorial. They will also find *United States of America*. Explain that these are all coins for the United States; coins from different countries will be different. Students may also give information about the color of pennies.

Extensions

On separate days introduce nickels, dimes, and quarters. Follow the same procedure as above and make a separate list for each coin. Post these lists in the classroom.

Add these books by Mary Hill to your classroom library: *Pennies*, *Nickels*, *Dimes*, and *Quarters*. These books are useful for helping students identify coins. Each book introduces a coin and is written for beginning readers.

Ideas for Parents

Read the suggested books in this lesson at home with your child. Give your child many opportunities to explore what is on coins and discuss the characteristics of coins. If your child struggles to identify pennies, nickels, dimes, and quarters, this is an essential lesson—coin rubbings can be fun to do at home too!

For further insights on helping your child with coin recognition, see the section, Additional Ideas for Parents, page 25. See also the Letter to the Parents, page 231.

The Matching Game
Coin identification practice for young learners

Overview

After students have looked closely at all four coins (see Lesson 1.2), they may need more opportunities to reaffirm coin identities. In this catchy game, students pull out coins from socks in the search for "monetary matches!" Students first play in a whole-group setting, with the teacher selecting a coin and asking students to pull from their coin-filled socks until they have a match. Students then play in pairs, ultimately reconvening as a group to process the experience, thinking about key questions such as "Which coins were easy to find? Which were more difficult?" and discovering the unique characteristic of a reeded edge on some coins. The game can be placed in a center for students to repeat in small-group exploration.

Economics Goals

Students will show:
▶ understanding of the Concept of Money by:
  • recognizing various forms of U.S. currency

Materials

sock, 1 per child (either children's or adults)

1 penny, 1 nickel, 1 dime, and 1 quarter in each sock

Time

1 class period

Teaching Insight:
Getting Socks
See page xxi for tips on collecting and using socks in your classroom.

Teaching Directions

Part 1: Introducing the Game

1. Give each child one sock and four coins (a penny, a nickel, a dime, and a quarter). Have students put coins into the sock. If coins are already in the sock, always start by having students take coins out to make sure they have all four coins.

2. As the teacher, begin by reaching into your sock and pulling out any coin. Say "my coin is a . . ." (whatever the coin is). Ask students to reach into their socks and try to find the same coin. Have students pull out the coin they think is a match and hold it so you can see it. You will notice that quarters are the easiest to find.

3. After the match has been made, have everyone return the coins to the sock. (Mathematicians would say we are sampling with replacement.) Play this game in a whole-group setting until you have identified each coin once or twice.

Part 2: Playing the Game

4. Next ask students to work in pairs. First one partner will reach in and pull out a coin. The other partner tries to match the coin with his or her coin pulled from the sock. Then partners trade tasks, with the second partner pulling out a coin and the first partner trying to match the coin.

Part 3: Processing the Game

5. After students have had an opportunity to play for a few minutes, stop the game and ask "Which coins were easy to find? Which were more difficult?" Be sure to ask why these coins were easier or more difficult to find. Have students place all four coins in front of them. Ask students to look at the coins and try to figure out what about the coins helps them identify them. (Expect to hear that quarters are larger, dimes are the smallest.)

6. Ask students to push the coins together and compare the thickness of the coins. Students should realize that quarters are the thickest and dimes are the thinnest. (It may be difficult for little fingers to find much difference.) Students should also discover that nickels and quarters are about the same thickness (nickels and quarters are easily confused by young students).

Key Questions

Which coins were easy to find? Why?

Which coins were more difficult to find? Why?

What about the coins helps you identify them?

Financial Fact

When a coin has those little ridges, it is called a reeded edge. Reeds were put on coins that were made of gold and silver so the edges couldn't be cut off without it being noticed. Pennies and nickels weren't considered important coins and weren't made of precious metals so they don't have any ridges.

7. Then ask students to pick up one coin at a time and run their fingernail against the edge of the coin. Ask them what they notice. Students should discover quarters and dimes have ridges around their edges. Nickels and pennies are smooth.

8. Add any additional information that helps identify coins to the four coin lists you created in Lesson 1.2.

Ideas for Parents

This matching game is a great means to involve your child in financial thinking at home. Especially play it if your child is unsure of coin identification. Play this game for a few minutes daily until identification becomes easier to your child. On the other hand, this lesson should be skipped for children who instantly recognize coins—go right to Lesson 1.4.

For further insights on helping your child with coin recognition, see the section, Additional Ideas for Parents, page 25. See also the Letter to the Parents, page 231.

A Penny a Day

An introduction to coin values for young learners

Overview

Over the period of a month, children fill a container with pennies. They then estimate the number of pennies in the container and begin counting pennies, inspired by *The Coin Counting Book*. This lesson is appropriate to use with all children who are starting to learn coin values and learning to count coins. This is a class routine that is best started at the first of a month. In first grade, the first full month of the school year is a good place to start. In kindergarten you may want to wait until after the first of the calendar year.

Common Core State Standards for Mathematics:

Counting and Cardinality   K.CC.1.4.5
- *Know number names and the count sequence*
- *Count to tell the number of objects*

Number and Operations in Base Ten   1.NBT.1.2.a.b.c
- *Extend the counting sequence*
- *Understand place value*

Number and Operations in Base Ten   2.NBT.2
- *Understand place value*

Measurement and Data   2.MD.8
- *Work with time and money*

Mathematics Goals

Students will:
- ▶ count by ones, fives, and tens
- ▶ use ten as a bundle of ones
- ▶ solve problems using money

Economics Goals

Students will show:
- ▶ understanding of the Concept of Money by:
  - • recognizing various forms of U.S. currency

Materials

1 clear container, large enough to hold 30 pennies

30 pennies

Literature Connections

The Coin Counting Book by Rozanne Lanczak Williams

Time

30 minutes (to prepare for this lesson, Step 1 needs to be done over the period of a month)

Teaching Directions

Part 1: Collecting Pennies Daily

1. On the first day of the month, ask a child to place one penny in the container. On each following school day, ask students to place one penny per day in the container. Don't count coins or work with them in any way until the end of the month. Do explain to students that they will be counting the coins after you have collected coins for the whole month.

Part 2: Estimating the Penny Collection

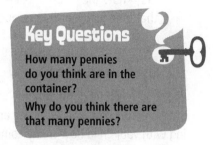

Key Questions

How many pennies do you think are in the container?

Why do you think there are that many pennies?

2. At the end of the month, ask students to estimate how many pennies are in the container. Many students will provide reasonable answers. Ask a child who said "thirty" or "thirty-one" to explain their estimate. Ask another child who gave a little less than thirty to explain their estimate. Expect a connection with the number of days in a month and the number of pennies in a jar. You may have some wildly high estimates.

3. After you have heard and talked about estimates, have students sit in a circle so everyone can see the pennies and count them. Make sure students can see the coins being counted. Students may notice the month has thirty or thirty-one days in it but there are fewer pennies. This is a good time to say that no pennies were put into the container on Saturdays or Sundays. Move the pennies as you count them to keep track of what has been counted, giving a good example of using one-to-one correspondence to keep track of the coins that have been counted.

Part 3: Reading and Exploring the Book

4. Read *The Coin Counting Book* by Rozanne Lanczak Williams. For the first reading, read the book completely without stopping. Then go back to the page that shows five pennies and one nickel.

5. Explain that a nickel is worth five pennies. Put pennies from the container into a line, similar to the illustrations in *The Coin Counting Book*, grouping the line into fives. Place a nickel by each group of five pennies. Demonstrate counting by fives while you point to nickels. Emphasize that you can count the pennies by ones or the nickels by fives and end up with the same amount.

6. Then go back to the page that shows ten pennies and one dime. Explain that a dime is worth ten pennies. Put pennies from the jar into a line, grouping the line into tens. Place a dime by each group of ten pennies. Demonstrate counting by tens while you point to dimes. Emphasize that you can count the pennies by ones or the dimes by tens and end up with the same amount.

7. Turn to the page that shows two nickels equals one dime. Line the coins up so students can see a connection between the pennies, nickels, and dimes. Count the coins by ones, fives, and tens. Encourage students to count with you. If you are counting alone when you first count these coins, repeat and request that students count with you.

Part 4: Repeating the Experience

8. When the counting and exchanging is done, empty the container and start the routine over again the first day of the next month. As the year passes, students may know the value of coins and the connection to the days in the month. At that time you can discontinue the routine.

Idea$ for Parent$

This lesson can be done at home in nearly the same way it is used in a classroom. Start a penny container at home and have your child add to it daily. Practice estimating with your child how many coins are in the container. Ask your child the key questions featured in the teaching directions. Read the corresponding book with your child, pointing out financial and mathematical concepts in much the same way the teacher would do so in a classroom.

For further insights on helping your child with coin recognition, see the section, Additional Ideas for Parents, page 25. See also the Letter to the Parents, page 231.

A Number a Day

A routine for young learners who can count money

Overview

This quick class routine gives children an opportunity to handle money on a daily basis. Students work individually or in small groups to build the corresponding calendar number with coins. They then convene as a whole group to discuss their strategies. Students are encouraged to think of additional ways of building the number, solving questions such as "What are the most coins you can use to build this number?" The lesson is appropriate to use with children who are able to count by ones, fives, and tens to one hundred.

Common Core State Standards for Mathematics:

Number and Operations in Base Ten   K.NBT.1
  • *Work with numbers 11–19 to gain foundations for place value*

Operations and Algebraic Thinking   1.OA.1.5
  • *Represent and solve problems involving addition and subtraction*
  • *Add and subtract within 20*

Operations and Algebraic Thinking   2.OA.1.2
  • *Represent and solve problems involving addition and subtraction*
  • *Add and subtract within 20*

Number and Operations in Base Ten   2.NBT.2.5.8
  • *Understanding place value*
  • *Use place value understanding and properties of operations to add and subtract*

Measurement and Data   2.MD.8
  • *Work with time and money*

Mathematics Goals

Students will:
▶ represent and solve problems involving addition and subtraction
▶ represent and solve problems involving money
▶ compose and decompose numbers

Time

15 minutes

Materials

chart paper or some means of displaying written lists for students to see

30 pennies, 10 nickels, 10 dimes, and 1 quarter for each student or group of students

Teaching Directions

Part 1: Building Numbers

1. Tell students this is the ___ day of school. Say, "Using pennies, nickels, dimes, and quarters, how many ways do you think we can build that number with coins?" Give students time to work on this problem either individually or in a small group.

2. Ask students to compare the ways they found to build the number with coins with others in their group.

Part 2: Discussing the Experience

3. After students have had time to look at each other's work, ask them to describe their work for the whole group. Record students' descriptions where everyone can see them (consider using chart paper). Ask, "What are the most coins you can use to build this number?" This gives you an opportunity to honor those students who counted by ones and used pennies.

Part 3: Solving Questions

4. Next, ask students to compare ideas in their groups and try to find the way to build the number using the least number of coins. (For the twenty-sixth day of school, the least would be built with one quarter and one penny.) Ask students to compare their findings and see how many different ways their group made this number in coins.

5. Then ask if anyone can describe if this number can be made with even numbers of dimes and nickels and pennies. Continue taking suggestions until many ways to make the number have been found.

6. Post the students' descriptions in the classroom.

> ### Key Questions
>
> How many ways do you think we can build that number with coins? Describe some of the ways.
>
> What are the most coins you can use to build this number?
>
> What ways can you build the number using the least number of coins?
>
> Can the number be made with even numbers of dimes, nickels, and pennies? Explain.

Extensions

Consider giving students directions to follow on different days, such as:

- Can this number be built with only dimes and pennies?
- Can this number be built using every coin at least once?
- Can you build with more dimes than nickels?
- Can you build with more nickels than dimes?
- Can you build this number with all dimes?

- What is the least amount of coins you can use?
- What is the greatest amount of coins you can use?

Ideas for Parents

You may want to modify this lesson to a one-on-one contest with you and your child. Choose a number (it can be a number corresponding to the date or any random number). Take turns building that number with coins. Make sure each new way is unique. You might want to agree that building with only pennies is one of the ways to build the number. Ask your child the key questions featured in the teaching directions. On a piece of paper, record in writing the different ways to build a number with coins. Consider using the suggested extensions.

For further insights on helping your child with coin recognition, see the section, Additional Ideas for Parents, page 25. See also the Letter to the Parents, page 231.

Race to a Quarter
Trading coins practice for young learners

Overview

Young children need many opportunities to think about the value of coins and make trades. One way is to provide opportunities for individual explorations during center or individual investigation time. This coin-trading game allows students to work in a group to count and trade coins. When the number of pennies in the supply container is limited, students are forced to make trades instead of accumulating pennies. See the "Extensions" section for an advanced version of this game (*Race to a Dollar*).

Common Core State Standards for Mathematics:

Number and Operations in Base Ten   1.NBT.1.2.a
- *Extend the counting sequence*
- *Understand place value*

Operations and Algebraic Thinking   1.OA.7
- *Work with addition and subtraction equations*

Number and Operations in Base Ten   2.NBT.2
- *Understand place value*

Measurement and Data 2.MD.8
- *Work with time and money*

Mathematics Goals

Students will:
- ▶ trade coins for equivalent values
- ▶ count groups of coins
- ▶ think of ten (dimes) as ten pennies

Time

15 minutes, after students have had an introduction to this game (the first day this game is played, allow time for a demonstration or sit with a small group and teach a few students at a time how to play)

Materials

For each group of players:
30 pennies, 10 nickels, 10 dimes, 1 quarter, 1 die

**Teaching Insight:
Sets of Coins**

For this game, limit the number of coins in the coin supply to thirty pennies, ten nickels, ten dimes, and one quarter. Place coins in a plastic container or plastic bag for each group of players. At the end of the class period, ask students to count the coins into the container. Remove the coins from workspaces before moving on to other classroom activities.

Teaching Directions

Part 1: Introducing the Game

1. Explain to students that they will be playing a game, *Race to a Quarter*, in which they will be thinking about the value of coins and making trades. Demonstrate this game by choosing two or three students to join you in a game while other students watch:

   a. Tell students that you are going to take turns rolling the die. The amount on the die tells you how many pennies to take.

   b. When it is your turn, you control the die and can make trades after you have tossed the die and taken pennies. If you have five pennies, you can trade them for one nickel. When you make a trade, you have to say what you are trading, such as "I am trading five pennies for one nickel" and hold the coins so everyone can see.

   c. When the trades are completed, pass the die to the next player. Players can trade only when it is their turn.

   d. The game continues until one player wins by trading coins for one quarter. (If other students have twenty-five cents but have not traded, the student trading first wins.)

Teaching Insight:
Coin Trading Rules
It is really common for young children to confuse coins, so it is important for everyone to agree with what is being traded. Students also learn from each other when the correct coins are traded.

Part 2: Playing the Game

2. Group students in random mixed-ability groups to play the game (different levels of understanding helps when students have questions identifying coins or remembering coin values). While students are playing, observe different groups. Informally assess how students work together, if they can identify coins, and if they know coin values. Answer questions students may have about counting or identifying coins.

Extensions

For an advanced version of *Race to a Quarter*, play *Race to a Dollar* (for experienced counters). For each group of players, you'll need thirty pennies, thirty nickels, thirty dimes, twenty-five quarters, one die, and one one-dollar bill or coin. Students roll the die, count pennies from the supply container, and make trades, just the same as they did in *Race to a Quarter*. The first student to be able to trade for a dollar wins.

Idea$ for Parent$

The *Race to a Quarter* game is enjoyed by children who fluently count money, as well as those who are still struggling with coin identification and values. This is a game that travels well and can be played while you and your child are waiting for an appointment or a meal in a restaurant. The game will help reinforce coin values, counting, and counting on from a different type of coin (for example, counting one dime, two nickels, and a penny: "ten, fifteen, twenty, twenty-one"). Children generally like this game and will want to play it over and over with you!

For further insights on helping your child with coin recognition, see the section, Additional Ideas for Parents, page 25. See also the Letter to the Parents, page 231.

What Is Money?

Formative Assessment

Economic and mathematical ideas that need to be assessed in this chapter are identification of coins and coin values. The ability to count nickels and dimes depends on a child's ability to count by fives and tens. Many young children need many money counting experiences before becoming proficient at counting groups of coins that are the same.

Coin identification, valuation, and money-counting skills can best be accomplished with quick one-on-one assessments. Use the following chart to assist you in knowing who needs to be assessed while students are involved in an investigation or small-group activity. Pull students aside one at a time or work with a small group of students playing a game like *Race to a Quarter*, or observe students as they work at those activities.

The results of these assessments may tell you that students need more class time spent on certain skills or that students are proficient and it is time to move on to other skills. You should be able to use this information while meeting with parents to explain how they can assist their children in learning to count money and identify coins. Also, recording when students identify and count coins helps in planning for future instruction.

Formative Assessment Checklist
Chapter 1 Lessons, What Is Money?

Student Name	Identifies Pennies	Identifies Nickels	Identifies Dimes	Identifies Quarters	Counts Pennies	Counts Dimes	Counts Nickels

Additional Idea$ for Parent$

Helping Your Child Be Financially Savvy with Coin Recognition

In exploring the question "What is money?," start by taking advantage of your child's natural curiosity. Let him or her see, touch, and handle coins from your pocket or purse at the end of the day. Identify the coins as your child handles them. For example, when your child holds a dime say, "That's a dime. It's worth ten cents." Keep your explanations simple and clear. Young children can also learn about the process of paying when they accompany you to a store or fast-food establishment. When small purchases are made, hand the money to your child to pay at the counter. Explain the process. Start by saying the amount of money needed and then counting the money into your child's hand. Keep it as simple as possible. For example, if you buy a dollar-store item, give your child a dollar bill plus coins to cover the tax. (Always be mindful that very young children should be supervised when handling coins, as coins might pose a choking problem.)

Use the lessons in Chapter 1 that fit your child's needs. When you are trying to decide which lessons to use, knowing what your child knows is important. If you aren't sure which lessons are appropriate for your child, start with the following quick assessment. Give your child this informal assessment to determine any need to work on coin recognition.

Parent-Child Assessment: Coin Recognition

Conduct this assessment informally by placing a collection of coins in your hand. (For five- to six-year-olds have pennies, nickels, and dimes. If your child is a first- or second-grade student, include quarters.) Tell your child to choose any coin. When your child is holding a coin, ask, "Do you know what that coin is called?" Then place aside (or ask your child to place aside) the coin that he or she just identified from the collection. Do the same process until all coins have been identified. Remember, you are assessing, not teaching. Refrain from responding with comments like "that's right" or "that's not a dime." If your child selects a nickel and calls it a quarter, make a mental note that your child needs more experience identifying nickels. If you correct your child by saying the correct coin name, you are disrupting the assessment process; the child might start to see the process as a guessing game—he or she makes a guess—if it's not correct, you'll say so. This guessing game makes it challenging to know if your child really knows a quarter is a quarter or if it's just a name that didn't work before (in which case the child will simply guess again).

Continue assessing (and refraining from teaching) until all coins in your collection have been set aside. At this stage, you should have a pretty good idea if your child can identify coins or if he or she needs more experiences.

Now return to the coins and give each coin the correct name. The assessment is over and it's the appropriate time to reinforce correct coin names. Keep this assessment and corrections light and pleasant for your child. Learning coin identities is a process—young children need to revisit coin identities many times before they know them.

For children who identify pennies, nickels, dimes, and quarters correctly, consider taking the assessment to the next level by asking how much each coin is worth.

My Reflections, Lesson Notes, and Ideas

CHAPTER 2

Where Do We Get Our Money?

Investigate Basic Concepts of Earning, Wanting, and Needing Money–From Allowances to the Tooth Fairy

Overview

In this chapter students explore concepts of earning, wanting, and needing money—further understanding why families and individuals cannot always have everything they want. Students consider money in contexts they are familiar with, from money they receive as an allowance to money the tooth fairy gives them.

Lessons 2.1 through **2.3** use the classic children's book *The Berenstain Bears' Trouble with Money* as a springboard for discussing the use and sources of money, including understanding financial figures of speech from "made of money" to "money grows on trees."

Lessons 2.4 through **2.6** introduce students to the use of the counting jar—a learning tool that in some ways mirrors the concept of a piggybank. These activities give students experience with estimating, recognizing, and counting collections of coins at several levels, as well as the opportunity to participate in problem-solving situations.

Lesson 2.7 introduces students to the classic children's book *Little Rabbit's Loose Tooth*, prompting students to think about a source of money they are likely familiar with—the tooth fairy—and collect data on how much money the tooth fairy has left Little Rabbit.

Lesson 2.8 builds on the mathematical side of money concepts in *Little Rabbit's Loose Tooth*, moving students into counting combinations of pennies and dimes while simultaneously continuing to reinforce an understanding of where money comes from and the need to use it sensibly.

The Lessons

Formative Assessment
59

Formative Assessment Checklist
60

Literature Used in This Chapter

The Berenstain Bears' Trouble with Money by Stan and Jan Berenstain

Little Rabbit's Loose Tooth by Lucy Bate

Additional Idea$ for Parent$

The Trouble with Money

An economics lesson for young learners

"When little bears spend every nickel and penny, the trouble with money is—they never have any!"

In the timeless children's book, *The Berenstain Bears' Trouble with Money,* Brother and Sister Bear find ways to get coins for the Astro Bear video game—learning valuable concepts about wanting, needing, saving, and spending money. This funny, realistic story provides a springboard for exploring the idea of allowances, earning and saving money, and common figures of speech we use when talking about money. The lesson opens with reading and exploring the book. Students then engage in a data collection activity in which they explore their own understanding of the sources of money and how they use it.

Mathematics Goals

Students will:
- ▶ solve simple compare problems involving information from graphs

Common Core State Standards for Mathematics:

Measurement and Data   K.MD.3
- *Classify objects and count the number of objects in each category*

Measurement and Data   1.MD.4
- *Represent and interpret data*

Measurement and Data   2.MD.10
- *Represent and interpret data*

Economics Goals

Students will show:
- ▶ understanding of the Concept of Earning Money by:
  - •discussing that work provides income to purchase goods and services
- ▶ understanding of the Concept of Goods and Services by:
  - •discussing that people save money for future goods and services
- ▶ understanding of the Concept of Wants and Needs by:
  - •explaining that individuals and families cannot have everything they want
  - •identifying examples of wanting more than we have
  - •explaining some of the consequences of unplanned spending

Materials

tag board or laminated colored construction paper, 2 pieces

sticky notes

clothespins, 1 per student

Literature Connections

The Berenstain Bears' Trouble with Money by Stan and Jan Berenstain

Time

1 class period

Teaching Directions

Part 1: Introducing the Book

1. Gather students in the whole-group area of your classroom. Before you start reading, show students the cover of the book *The Berenstain Bears' Trouble with Money* and ask, "Why do you think this book is called *Trouble with Money*?" Give students time to think and then share their predictions.

Part 2: Reading the Book

2. Read the book to students, making sure they can see the illustrations.

3. After you have read the story to students, ask the key questions (Set 1).

4. Give students opportunities to describe the sources of their own personal money. Continue asking more questions (Set 2).

5. Remind students of the change in the little bears and how they began earning money. Ask more key questions (Set 3).

Part 3: Collecting Data

6. Tell students, "We are going to do some quick data collection." Prepare two different colors of tag board or laminated colored construction paper. Use sticky notes to indicate which piece of tag board is "yes" and which is "no" or other responses. Give each student a clothespin; explain to students that they will be answering questions by clipping their clothespin to the tag board that matches their response.

Teaching Insight: Picture Books

When reading picture books in whole-group settings, consider using a document camera or some form of technology that will project the illustrations for the whole class to more easily see.

Key Questions

Set 1

Where did Brother and Sister Bear usually get their money?

Do any of you get money as presents? From grandparents? From doing chores for a neighbor? Describe.

Key Questions

Set 2

At the beginning of the story what did Brother and Sister Bear do when they got money?

What did they do with their money near the end of the book?

Key Questions

Set 3

What did Papa Bear mean when he said the little bears were caring too much for money?

When Papa Bear said some things are more important than money, what did he mean?

Ask the following data collection questions shown here. Use these questions in one day or over several days.

Part 4: Processing the Data

7. After each collection of data, gather students in a whole-group setting and discuss the key questions.

Extensions

For students who have had many experiences in collecting data, ask them to conduct their own surveys linking personal information to the question "Where do we get our money?" In partners, have students create a question, survey their fellow classmates, and then display the data on a large sheet of paper for everyone to see.

Ideas for Parents

Read the book in this lesson at home with your child. Encourage discussions about earning money, receiving allowances, and spending money. Instead of collecting data as this lesson instructs, talk with your child about the Data Collection Questions listed in the directions, one question at a time. Give your child an opportunity to respond quickly by sitting and standing for the yes and no answers.

For further insights on allowances, see the section, Additional Ideas for Parents, page 61. See also the Letter to the Parents, page 232.

Data Collection Questions

If someone gave you money today, what would you do? Spend it? Or save it?

Have you ever lost or misplaced money? Yes or no?

If you saw a coin on the ground, would you pick it up? Yes or no?

Do you ever buy things you don't want or need when you get home? Yes or no?

Do you ever buy someone else presents when you get money? Yes or no?

Key Questions

What do you notice about our data?

What would someone coming into our classroom know about us when they see our data?

Which had the most responses?

Which had the least responses?

How many more/fewer responses were there?

Does Money Grow on Trees?

Understanding financial figures of speech for young learners

Overview

In this lesson, students explore the meaning of four commonly used figures of speech when talking about money—*made of money, money grows on trees, saving for a rainy day,* and *nest egg.* Understanding these figures of speech helps students further investigate where we get—and don't get—our money. Teach this lesson after students have read and are familiar with the book *The Berenstain Bears' Trouble with Money* (see Lesson 2.1).

Economics Goals

Students will show:

▶ understanding of the Concept of Wants and Needs by:
- explaining that individuals and families cannot have everything they want
- identifying examples of wanting more than we have
- explaining why wanting more than we have requires people to make choices

Materials

Figure of Speech Recording Sheets (Reproducibles 2.2a, 2.2b, 2.2c, and 2.2d), 1 copy for each student

Time

1 class period

Literature Connections

The Berenstain Bears' Trouble with Money by Stan and Jan Berenstain

Teaching Directions

Part 1: Introducing Figures of Speech

1. Gather students in the whole-group area of your classroom. Point out to students that in the book *The Berenstain Bears' Trouble with Money,* Papa Bear used several figures of speech when talking about money. Explain that adults use figures of speech to illustrate what they are thinking.

Part 2: Exploring Figures of Speech

2. Ask students to write or draw to show what they understand when they hear the financial figures of speech. For each figure of speech, give students a copy of the corresponding recording sheet (see Reproducibles 2.2a through 2.2d). Read each figure of speech. Don't allow students to look at the book illustrations while they are completing this assignment.

Teaching Insight:
Distributing the Reproducibles
Ask each student to illustrate all four figures of speech or, alternatively, distribute the recording sheets so that each figure of speech is illustrated by a share of the students.

Part 3: Discussing Figures of Speech

3. After students finish their recording sheets, display the sheets in the classroom or assemble them into a book on figures of speech.

4. Gather students in a whole-group setting. Look at students' explanations and allow students to describe what they were thinking. Follow student discussion with the real meanings of these figures of speech.

Financial Figures of Speech

Made of money

Money grows on trees

Saving for a rainy day

Nest egg

Teaching Insight:
Spendthrift vs. Miser
In the book *The Berenstain Bears' Trouble with Money,* Papa Bear was first concerned about the cubs' "spendthrift way with money." Later he said they were turning into misers. Discuss the meaning of *spendthrift* and *miser* with students. Point out that these two words are opposites of each other.

Idea$ for Parent$

Read the book in this lesson at home with your child. Encourage discussions about the financial figures of speech targeted in this lesson. Explore other money-related figures of speech that you know. For example:

- a penny saved is a penny earned
- don't count your chickens before they are hatched
- a stitch in time saves nine

For further insights on allowances, see the section, Additional Ideas for Parents, page 61. See also the Letter to the Parents, page 232.

Figure of Speech

Student Name_____

Write or draw your understanding of the following figure of speech.

Made of money

"You must think I'm made of money!" —Papa Bear

Reproducible 2.2b

Figure of Speech

Student Name_____

Write or draw your understanding of the following figure of speech.

Money grows on trees

"You must think money grows on trees!" —Papa Bear

Figure of Speech

Student Name_____

Write or draw your understanding of the following figure of speech.

Saving for a rainy day

"That's what life is about … saving for a rainy day." —Papa Bear

Figure of Speech

Student Name_____

Write or draw your understanding of the following figure of speech.

Nest egg

"That money can be your nest egg." —Papa Bear

Do You Get an Allowance?

Practice in collecting data for young learners

Overview

In this quick lesson students are prompted to think about another source of money they are likely familiar with: receiving an allowance. Students collect and explore data for the question "Do you get an allowance?" Teach this lesson after students have read and are familiar with the book *The Berenstain Bears' Trouble with Money* (see Lesson 2.1).

Common Core State Standards for Mathematics:

Measurement and Data   K.MD.3
- *Classify objects and count the number of objects in each category*

Measurement and Data   1.MD.4
- *Represent and interpret data*

Measurement and Data   2.MD.10
- *Represent and interpret data*

Mathematics Goals

Students will:
- ▶ solve simple compare problems involving information from graphs

Economics Goals

Students will show:
- ▶ understanding of the Concept of Goods and Services by:
  - •discussing that people save money for future goods and services

Materials

Do You Get an Allowance? Graph (Reproducible 2.3), copy enlarged so entire class can see it

Literature Connections

The Berenstain Bears' Trouble with Money by Stan and Jan Berenstain

Time

15 minutes

Teaching Directions

Part 1: Discussing Allowances

1. Gather students in the whole-group area of your classroom. Remind students of the book *The Berenstain Bears' Trouble with Money*. Refer back to the page where Mama Bear was becoming concerned about the little bears' spending habits and suggested they should have a regular allowance. She said she wanted Brother and Sister Bear to learn to use money sensibly, "to save, to plan ahead." Ask students, "What do you think Mama Bear meant?" Give students time to think and discuss.

2. Introduce students to the *Do You Get an Allowance? Graph* (see Reproducible 2.3). Explain to students that you want them to mark the graph by writing their name in the space under "yes" or "no" in answer to the question "Do you get an allowance?"

3. Ask students, "What is an allowance?" Listen to several students and make sure there are no questions about what an allowance is before they begin marking the graph.

Part 2: Completing and Discussing the Graph

4. Give students time to mark the graph. When students have finished, reconvene as a whole group and ask key questions.

Students may or may not be able to draw a conclusion from this information, but you will know how many of your students are receiving an allowance and are beginning to manage their own money. See also the Letter to the Parents, page 232, for ideas for parents on taking advantage of the learning opportunities involved with giving children allowances.

Key Questions

Which column has the most responses?

Which column has the least responses?

Are there more students who get allowances or more students who do not receive allowances?

How many more students (did or did not) receive an allowance?

Ideas for Parents

Read the book in this lesson at home with your child. Encourage discussions about giving and receiving allowances. Ask your child to think of five or more friends or relatives who are near your child's age. Have your child ask each of these individuals, "Do you get an allowance?" Discuss the information your child collects.

For further insights on allowances, see the section, Additional Ideas for Parents, page 61. See also the Letter to the Parents, page 232.

Do You Get an Allowance? Graph

Yes	No

Introducing the Counting Jar

A counting lesson for young learners

Overview

In this lesson students are introduced to the valuable and simple learning tool, the counting jar—which in some ways mirrors the concept of a piggybank. Counting jar activities provide another context for reinforcing an understanding of money, where it comes from, and the need to use it sensibly. Students have an opportunity to estimate the number of pennies in a jar, practice counting the pennies, and bump into the idea that the quantity of pennies stays the same, even if you skip count by another number. Students then take the activity to a problem-solving level, comparing the number of students in the class to the number of pennies in the jar through several engaging problem-solving situations.

Common Core State Standards for Mathematics:

Counting and Cardinality   K.CC.1.2.3.4.a.b.c.5
- *Know number names and the count sequence*
- *Count to tell the number of objects*

Number and Operations in Base Ten   1.NBT.1.2.a
- *Extend the counting sequence*
- *Understand place value*

Number and Operations in Base Ten   2.NBT.2
- *Understand place value*

Measurement and Data   2.MD.8
- *Work with time and money*

Mathematics Goals

Students will:
- ▶ count to know how many
- ▶ count by ones, fives, and tens
- ▶ solve problems involving money

Time

25 minutes

Materials

counting jar
coins

**Teaching Insight:
Coins**

For young children, for this lesson use pennies and limit the quantity to five more or less than the number of students in your class. For older students, consider using nickels, dimes, and so forth.

Teaching Directions

Part 1: Estimating

1. Put one type of coins into a jar (see the Teaching Insight near the Materials list; these directions refer to the use of pennies). Gather students in the whole-group area of your classroom. Tell students that this is the counting jar. Ask students to estimate how many pennies are in the jar. Honor all estimates. Ask a few children how they decided on a number. If a child parrots another child's estimate, ask him or her to explain why they chose that amount.

2. After estimating, count the pennies. Make sure every student can see as you count. You may want to ask a student to count the coins for you.

Part 2: Exploring Grouping Methods

3. Ask students, "Can you count the pennies any other way?" Depending on experience, students may be able to count pennies by fives or tens. Ask students, "How many pennies will there be if you count by fives?"

4. Recount the pennies using whichever grouping method was decided.

Part 3: Trading Coins

5. When you've finished counting by fives, remind students that a nickel is worth five pennies so you could trade each group of five pennies for one nickel. Trade the coins and count again. When you have fewer than five coins remaining, model counting on by saying "five, ten, fifteen, twenty, twenty-one, twenty-two, and twenty-three. . . ." Be sure to explain that when you are counting more than one type of coin, a very effective strategy is to start counting with the coin that is worth the most.

**Teaching Insight:
Estimating**
Do not be surprised if your students give you estimates that are different from the amount of coins just counted. This is an indication of their development and tells you that they need many more experiences.

Key Questions

Can you count the pennies any other way?

How many pennies will there be if you count by fives? Tens?

**Teaching Insight:
Grouping Methods**
When you recount the pennies by fives (or whichever grouping method your class decides on), some students will be surprised that the number is the same as when you counted the pennies by ones. These students need more experience and should be given many more opportunities to count objects in more than one way.

**Teaching Insight:
Repeated Experiences**
For young students who are counting pennies, vary the number of pennies and repeat this counting jar experience every few weeks. Watch for better estimates as students have more experience.

Part 4: Solving Problems

6. After several rounds of estimating and counting pennies in the counting jar, ask students the problem-solving questions.

7. After listening to students explain their thinking, distribute the coins in the jar. Count the coins held by students. Then count the coins left in the jar. Relate the number of coins left in the jar to the number of students in the class. For example say, "We gave pennies to eighteen students. We have four pennies left in the jar. We have twenty-two pennies in all."

Extensions

Consider this extension if students are ready to make connections to equations. As they answer the problem-solving questions, write corresponding equations for everyone to see. Alternatively, ask students to work in pairs to write equations. For example, if there are twenty-three coins in the counting jar and twenty-one students in class that day, you might write *23 – 21 = 2*, to match the explanation that there are twenty-one students in class and twenty-three pennies; the difference is two.

Problem-Solving Questions

If I take the coins from the jar and start with the person sitting next to me, do I have enough coins to give one penny to each student? Why or why not?

If I don't have enough pennies to give everyone a penny, who will be the last person to receive a penny? Explain your thinking.

If I only have enough pennies to give one penny to each student, how many pennies will be left in the jar after I have given a penny to each student? Explain your thinking.

Ideas for Parents

You can use this lesson at home with your child just as it is written here. Young children need many experiences with counting before becoming fluent counters. Be sure to watch your child count. Does he or she move each penny to keep track of what has already been counted? Does your child know the rote counting sequence? If not, reduce the number of pennies and begin counting again. Repeat the counting jar activity, increasing the number of pennies and reinforcing the rote counting sequence. It is not unusual for students to believe that the number of pennies will change if the skip counting sequence is changed. The experience of counting by more than one way is important.

For further insights on allowances, see the section, Additional Ideas for Parents, page 61. See also the Letter to the Parents, page 232.

How Much Money Is in the Counting Jar?

A counting lesson for more experienced counters

Overview

This lesson is appropriate for helping students count by ones, fives, and tens. In this lesson students revisit the counting jar introduced in Lesson 2.4. Counting jar activities provide another context for reinforcing an understanding of money, where it comes from, and the need to use it sensibly. Working individually or in pairs, students estimate how many coins are in a jar and identify the type of coin and the coin's value. The jar is left for students to work with throughout the week. Students complete a recording sheet and convene at the end of the week to show and explain their thinking and discover how close their estimates are to what is actually in the jar.

Mathematics Goals

Students will:
▶ count to know how many
▶ count by ones, fives, and tens
▶ solve problems involving money
▶ work with equal groups of objects to gain foundations for multiplication

Common Core State Standards for Mathematics:

Number and Operations in Base Ten   1.NBT.1.2.a
• *Extend the counting sequence*
• *Understand place value*

Number and Operations in Base Ten   2.NBT.2
• *Understand place value*

Measurement and Data   2.MD.8
• *Work with time and money*

Operations and Algebraic Thinking   2.OA.4
• *Work with equal groups of objects to gain foundations for multiplication*

Time

35 minutes

Materials

counting jar

coins (nickels or dimes)

How Much Money Is in the Counting Jar? Recording Sheet (Reproducible 2.5), 1 copy per student or pair of students

Teaching Directions

Part 1: Introducing and Completing the Estimation

1. Remind students of the counting jar they used in Lesson 2.4. Explain to students that there is now a new number of coins in it that they will need to estimate. Each student needs to estimate how many coins are in a jar and identify the type of coin and the coin's value. Emphasize that students can shake the jar, look at the jar, count through the jar, but they cannot open the jar and remove any coins.

2. Let students know that you want to see how they figure out the total value of the coins. Show students Reproducible 2.5. Explain that each student will need to complete the recording sheet. Give students the opportunity to work on this alone or with a partner. Everyone needs to complete one recording sheet, even if she or he works with a partner.

3. Explain that you will be leaving the jar and copies of the recording sheet in a designated part of the classroom for an extended period of time. Place a pile of recording sheets near the counting jar. Specify a collection place where students place their completed recording sheets.

4. Let students ask questions about the assignment. There may be some confusion about figuring out the value. Leave this assignment open-ended. Students' work may reveal that they counted by fives (if the coins are nickels) or they used an arithmetic solution.

**Teaching Insight:
Giving Students Time**
For children who have had experience in counting coins, introduce the counting jar of coins early in the week. Leave this as a project for students to do during the next few days. Giving an extended time allows students time to closely look at the coins in the jar.

Part 2: Processing the Experience

5. At the end of the week, gather students in the whole-group area of your classroom. Open the counting jar and count the coins. Make sure all students can see as you count the coins. Give students opportunities to explain how they found the value. Start this sharing by asking if anyone would be willing to talk about their thinking when they completed the sheet. Ask if anyone thought about it in another way.

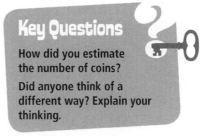

Key Questions

How did you estimate the number of coins?

Did anyone think of a different way? Explain your thinking.

Extensions

Revisit this lesson using the same jar but now with a different number of coins in the jar. For example, if you used nickels the first time, use dimes when you repeat this experience.

Ideas for Parents

You can use this lesson at home with your child just as it is written here; place the counting jar and recording sheet somewhere that's accessible to your child on a daily basis. Allow your child to revisit his or her thinking throughout the period of a week or month. Allot time to convene and discuss the experience with your child. This lesson is appropriate if your child can count by ones, fives, and tens. If your child cannot skip count by fives and tens, save this lesson for another time.

For further insights on allowances, see the section, Additional Ideas for Parents, page 61. See also the Letter to the Parents, page 232.

How Much Money Is in the Counting Jar?
Recording Sheet

Student's Name _____

Estimate the number of coins in the jar. Answer the following to explain your thinking.

My estimate is: _____

The types of coins in the jar are _____

Each coin is worth _____ cents.

Based on my estimate, I think the coins in the jar are worth:
_____

Show your work below.

From *Why Can't I Have Everything? Teaching Today's Children to Be Financially and Mathematically Savvy, Grades PreK–2* by Jane Crawford. © 2011 by Scholastic Inc. Permission granted to photocopy for nonprofit use in a classroom or similar place dedicated to face-to-face educational instruction.

Counting Jars for Small Groups

A counting investigation for young learners

Overview

Young children need many opportunities to count. One way is to provide opportunities for individual explorations during center or individual investigation time. This counting investigation continues the idea of using a counting jar (see Lessons 2.4 and 2.5), this time giving students the opportunity to work individually or with a partner to count pennies. Counting jar activities provide another context for reinforcing an understanding of money, where it comes from, and the need to use it sensibly.

Mathematics Goals

Students will:
- ▶ count to know how many

Common Core State Standards References:

Counting and Cardinality   K.CC.1.2.3.4.a.b.c.5
- *Know number names and the count sequence*
- *Count to tell the number of objects*

Number and Operations in Base Ten   1.NBT.1.2.a
- *Extend the counting sequence*
- *Understand place value*

Materials

several small empty containers, each labeled with a number (*3, 4, 5, 6, 7, 8, 9, 10, 11, 12, 13, 14, 15, 16, 17, 18, 19,* and *20*)

jars of approximately 100 pennies each, 1 per student or pair of students

Time

20 minutes

Teaching Directions

Part 1: Demonstrating the Activity

1. Have students work individually or in partners at tables or centers. Each student or pair of students needs a jar with pennies and at least five empty containers labeled with numbers.

2. Demonstrate the activity; students first look at the number written on one of their empty containers. The number shows the number of pennies students need to count into the empty container. If the number is ten, their container should have ten pennies in it when they are finished. When students have filled five of the empty containers, they ask someone at their table to check their counting by recounting the pennies in their containers.

Part 2: Doing the Activity

3. Have students work through the activity. Circulate, observing how students are counting. Consider the items in the teacher checklist in your observations.

   Make note of students who still need to be assessed or reassessed and check for identification and counting of coins. Use the chart at the end of this chapter, page 60, to record assessment results.

4. When students are finished and it is time to clean up, encourage students to be diligent in finding all the coins that were originally in the jars. Have students check their chairs and all around their tables for any coins that may have fallen on the floor. Students should empty all pennies from the labeled containers into the original jar.

Idea$ for Parent$

This lesson provides another opportunity for children to count. You can use this lesson at home with your child just as it is written here; have your child work on the activity individually or with siblings. Make sure you are available when your child is ready to have her or his counting checked (Step 3). If you don't have jars at home, use sheets of paper or small paper plates with the numbers written on them.

For further insights on allowances, see the section, Additional Ideas for Parents, page 61. See also the Letter to the Parents, page 232.

Teacher Checklist: Counting

Does the student use one-to-one correspondence when counting pennies?

Does the student understand that the last number said is the quantity of pennies counted?

Does the student know the rote counting sequence to this number?

Does the student "tag" as he or she counts, saying the number name while touching each penny?

Teaching Insight: Checking the Counts

When students are ready to have their counting checked, this is a good time to put a helper or volunteer in place at the tables to check the containers. If there are no volunteers in the classroom, have students recount each others' coins.

Teaching Insight: Coin Supplies

At this time, making sure that the exact number of pennies have been returned to the original jars will take too much time. Make a show of putting the money away in a safe place and praise students for returning all coins to their original jars. You may lose some coins in the process of counting; before the next center time, make sure each coin jar has enough coins for students to have an adequate amount for counting.

How Much Money Did the Tooth Fairy Leave?

A graphing lesson for young learners

Overview

"I have a tooth in my chocolate ice cream!" said Little Rabbit.

Little Rabbit's Loose Tooth is a quality piece of timeless literature; it's won the International Reading Association Children's Book Council Children's Choice award and a California Young Reader Medal. In this story, Little Rabbit loses a tooth and leaves it for the tooth fairy. The story's reference to pennies and dimes provides a springboard for encouraging students to figure out how much money is ultimately left under Little Rabbit's pillow. Students then chart their answers in a bar graph.

Common Core Standards for Mathematics:

Measurement and Data   K.MD.3
- *Classify objects and count the number of objects in each category*

Measurement and Data 1.MD.4
- *Represent and interpret data*

Measurement and Data 2.MD.10
- *Represent and interpret data*

Mathematics Goals

Students will:
- ▶ solve simple compare problems involving information from graphs

Economics Goals

Students will show:
- ▶ understanding of the Concept of Money by:
  - •recognizing various forms of U.S. currency

Materials

sticky notes, 1 per student

marker or crayon, 1 per student

1 dime

1 penny

Time

1 class period

Literature Connections

Little Rabbit's Loose Tooth by Lucy Bate

Teaching Directions

Part 1: Introducing the Book

1. Place a sticky note over the last page of *Little Rabbit's Loose Tooth* to stop you before reading it aloud to students. Gather students in the whole-group area of your classroom. Tell students that you are going to read the classic children's book *Little Rabbit's Loose Tooth.* Ask, "What do you know about loose teeth?" Children who have ever had a loose tooth can describe the whole process of wiggling and eventually losing a tooth.

Part 2: Reading the Book

2. Begin reading *Little Rabbit's Loose Tooth* aloud to students, making sure everyone can see the illustrations. There is a page where Little Rabbit asks her mother if she will get a dime or a penny from the tooth fairy. Little Rabbit says that a dime is smaller than a penny. Mother Rabbit explains that a dime is smaller but is worth more. She says that a dime is worth ten pennies. This is an opportunity to talk to students about the relative size of pennies and dimes; reaffirm that dimes are worth more than pennies. Have a penny and dime on hand to show.

Part 3: Building the Graph

3. Stop the story before you read the last page (your sticky note will remind you!). Ask students, "How much money do you think Little Rabbit found under her pillow?" Give each student a sticky note and a marker or crayon. Ask students to write on their sticky note how much money they think Little Rabbit found under her pillow. When all amounts have been written (but not shared), ask, "Who thought Little Rabbit received one penny?" Ask those students who wrote "1 cent" on their sticky note to bring it up and place it where everyone can see it (a board, etc.). Then ask about a nickel, then a dime—continuing until every student's sticky note response is posted, forming part of a classroom graph. To do this, you'll need to stack like sticky-note responses above each other, building a bar graph. Your graph may look something like Figure 2–1 if there is a wide variety of opinions.

> **Teaching Insight:**
> **The Tooth Fairy**
> During this lesson *never ever* say whether or not the tooth fairy is real. Many young children and their families enjoy this custom. A few families may not have visits from the tooth fairy, but we need to make sure not to ruin the fun for families that do. Some of your students may not have had visits from the tooth fairy if they have not begun to lose teeth. Be sure to explain that they will know when they have a loose tooth and if they haven't lost a tooth yet, it will happen naturally at the right time. Students should not pull teeth just to get a visit from a tooth fairy. Pulling a tooth that is not ready to be pulled could hurt! Parents and dentists know when teeth are ready to come out.

> **Teaching Insight:**
> **Picture Books**
> When reading picture books in whole-group settings, consider using a document camera or some form of technology that will project the illustrations for the whole class to more easily see.

		▓				
		▓				
▓		▓	▓			
▓		▓				
▓	▓	▓			▓	
Penny	Nickel	Dime	Quarter	Half-Dollar	Dollar	

Figure 2–1 Bar Graph for "What do you think Little Rabbit found under her pillow?"

4. When students have finished marking the graph, consider asking the key questions shown here.

5. After you've asked and discussed the key questions, finish reading the story. Students may have stories of loose teeth and money received from tooth fairies following the reading of this story; consider concluding by having some students share their personal stories and/or experiences with the tooth fairy.

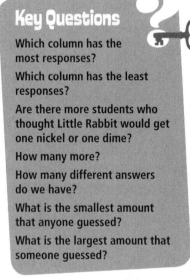

Key Questions

Which column has the most responses?

Which column has the least responses?

Are there more students who thought Little Rabbit would get one nickel or one dime?

How many more?

How many different answers do we have?

What is the smallest amount that anyone guessed?

What is the largest amount that someone guessed?

Teaching Insight:
The Term *Range*

The *range* is something that kindergarten and first-grade children are seldom asked. It is never required and shouldn't be assessed. It is OK for students to become comfortable with the term *range* and to develop vocabulary that includes *range*.

Teaching Insight:
The Term *Mode*
Young children can also begin to understand and use the graphing language of *mode*. The mode is the column in a bar graph with the most. Even young children can tell which one has the most. In the graph in Figure 2–1 the *mode* would be the dime.

Teaching Insight:
More About *Range* and *Mode*
The words *range* and *mode* are vocabulary used in statistics.

The *range* is the difference between the lowest and highest value in a set of numbers. It is found by ordering the numbers, starting with the smallest value and ending with the largest value. The range is found by subtracting the smallest number from the largest number.

For young children, a task associated with *range* would be to identify the lowest value and the highest value when talking about classroom graphs, without subtracting to find the difference between those two values. Identifying those two values requires no arithmetic operation. Even young children, who are not doing number operations, can use the word *range* and start developing an understanding before being formally assessed. As students become more proficient with subtraction, finding the difference and connecting that value to the word *range* is a better possibility

The *mode* is the value in a set of numbers that repeats most often. There can be more than one mode. If no number repeats more than once in any set of numbers, then there is no mode for that set of numbers. If there are two sets of numbers that repeat the most, both sets of numbers are the mode.

Building vocabulary to include an understanding of range and mode is generally not required in preK through second grade. There is no reason to avoid using this math vocabulary simply because it isn't required. If we can ask students what the lowest and highest numbers are on our graph, we can connect the word *range* in context while graphing. When students identify which happened the most, it is appropriate to attach the word *mode*.

Idea$ for Parent$

To adapt this lesson for home use, stop reading the book as indicated in Step 3. Ask your child, "What do you think Little Rabbit will find under her pillow?" Refer to the sample graph given in the lesson (Figure 2–1). Ask your child the key questions (see the list in Step 4) using the sample graph as reference.

For further insights on allowances, see the section, Additional Ideas for Parents, page 61. See also the Letter to the Parents, page 232.

Counting Combinations of Pennies and Dimes

Practice counting on for young learners

Overview

This lesson is appropriate to use with children who are able to rote count to one hundred and count by tens. In this lesson, students work together with a partner to count coin combinations of pennies and dimes. The lesson gives students an opportunity to become fluent in counting on while simultaneously continuing to reinforce an understanding of where money comes from and the need to use it sensibly. Teach this lesson after students have read and are familiar with the book *Little Rabbit's Loose Tooth* (see Lesson 2.7).

Common Core Standards for Mathematics:

Number and Operations in Base Ten   1.NBT.1.2.a.b.c
 • *Extend the counting sequence*
 • *Understand place value*

Number and Operations in Base Ten   2.NBT.2.8
 • *Understand place value*
 • *Use place value understanding and properties of operations to add and subtract*

Measurement and Data   2.MD.8
 • *Work with time and money*

Mathematics Goals

Students will:
 ▶ Count to know how many
 ▶ Count by ones and tens
 ▶ Solve problems involving money

Economics Goals

Students will show:
 ▶ understanding of the Concept of Money by:
  • recognizing various forms of U.S. currency

Materials

6 dimes and 6 pennies in a container for each student

Time

20 minutes

Literature Connections

Little Rabbit's Loose Tooth by Lucy Bate

Teaching Directions

Part 1: Introducing the Counting of Combinations

1. Remind students of the book they read in Lesson 2.7. Refer back to the page in *Little Rabbit's Loose Tooth* where Mother Rabbit gives Little Rabbit an envelope for her tooth. Mother Rabbit explains that a dime is worth ten pennies.

2. Give each student a container containing six dimes and six pennies. Ask students to take out two dimes and two pennies. Explain that you want to count these coins. Ask, "Who can explain how much a dime is worth?" Make sure everyone hears again that a dime is worth ten cents. Ask, "Who can explain how much a penny is worth?" Make sure everyone hears that a penny is worth one cent.

3. Tell students that you want to count two dimes and two pennies. Demonstrate counting this coin combination by pointing to one dime and saying "I always start with the coin that is worth the most when I count coins." Then count, "Ten, twenty, twenty-one, twenty-two." Ask students to count two dimes and two pennies to each other in their group.

Part 2: Counting Combinations

4. Tell students you want them to work with a partner. Students choose different combinations of pennies and dimes to count. As students are counting coins, move around the room, assisting students who need support in counting on.

Teaching Insight:
Counting On
Counting on from tens to ones is an advanced counting skill. Young children may find this difficult and may need many experiences in counting money before counting on becomes routine.

Extensions

Dimes and pennies are the easiest coins to practice counting on. If a child is fluently counting on from tens, increase the number of dimes. Following that, exchange the dimes for nickels, giving students an opportunity to skip count by fives and then count on by ones. Counting on using dimes, nickels, and pennies is a sophisticated skill and should follow both counting by dimes and pennies and counting by nickels and pennies.

Ideas for Parents

This lesson is appropriate if your child is able to rote count to one hundred and count by tens. If your child is just learning to count by tens, this is a good place to start. Make sure there is an understanding that a dime is worth ten cents. Slowly count, moving the dime you are counting to demonstrate keeping track of what has been counted. Have your child count with you. Repeat. Counting on is a sophisticated skill that every child must eventually master. For further insights on allowances, see the section, Additional Ideas for Parents, page 61. See also the Letter to the Parents, page 232.

CHAPTER 2
Where Do We Get Our Money?

Formative Assessment

In this chapter students were given opportunities to count coins, including pennies and dimes, together. Counting on is a sophisticated skill. It requires that a child count by tens (or fives) and then continue to count by ones to find the total.

Economic and mathematical assessments of identifying coins and telling coin values should continue. Use Reproducible 2 to keep track of student's money-counting skills.

Formative Assessment Checklist
Chapter 2 Lessons, Where Do We Get Our Money?

Student Name	Identifies Pennies	Identifies Nickels	Identifies Dimes	Identifies Quarters	Counts Pennies	Counts Nickels	Counts Dimes	Counts Quarters

Where Do We Get Our Money?

Additional Idea$ for Parent$

Helping Your Child Be Financially Savvy with Allowances

A valuable step in exploring the question "Where do we get our money?" is to give your child an allowance. An allowance is an important means of helping children explore the concepts of earning, wanting, and needing money—further understanding why families and individuals cannot always have everything they want. If you don't already give an allowance, consider doing so, timing it such that it coincides with the beginning of school. Consider some of the questions below if you are just beginning to give an allowance.

If your purpose in giving an allowance is to give your child an experience in managing money, there is no reason to tie it to chores. If you have chores you want your child to do and hope a work ethic will develop, you may want to connect an allowance to chores. If you want to periodically increase your child's allowance, consider doing so near birthdays or the first of the calendar year. Whatever you decide, always be consistent.

When you begin giving an allowance, vary the way you pay. For example, if the allowance is one dollar, give a dollar bill one week. The next week, pay the allowance in quarters. The following week, pay all in dimes. If your child is just learning to recognize coins and count money, make the counting process part of the allowance.

After starting to pay an allowance, give your child an opportunity to shop. Be prepared for your child to spend his or her first allowance completely. If your child spends it foolishly, stay quiet and let her or him make the decisions. When you are in a store and your child asks for something, ask, "Do

Questions to Consider When Giving an Allowance

How much money should I give?

How should I pay?

When should I pay?

How often should I pay?

Should the payments be linked to jobs around the house?

Do I give an allowance to older and younger siblings?

Do I pay everyone the same amount or do older children receive more?

What do I want to teach my child about managing this money?

How will I handle requests for money when my child has an allowance?

you have your allowance still?" This is a great time to talk about making decisions and how to make an allowance last until the next payday. Sometimes a good lesson is taught by suffering the consequences of spending foolishly. Always understand this is a learning process and not a punishment—important learning opportunities shouldn't be missed because an allowance was spent foolishly.

See also the Letter to the Parents, page 232.

My Reflections, Lesson Notes, and Ideas

CHAPTER 3

Do We Have Enough Money?

Understand the Value of Money—Focusing on Trading It, and Giving and Receiving Change

Overview

In this chapter students deepen their understanding of the value of money, gaining practice in trading it and giving and receiving change—ultimately realizing that sometimes having everything means being left with nothing! Students are also introduced to new items—from the value of a half-dollar **(Lesson 3.1)** to sales tax **(Lesson 3.2)**.

Mathematically, students count money, collect data, write equations, find combinations (how many ways can you make twenty-five cents?), think about equivalent equations, and solve problems in monetary contexts—leading to better algebraic understanding in the future.

In **Lesson 3.3** students go on a penny hunt, using their newfound treasures as counters on ten-frames.

In **Lesson 3.4** students help the main character in *A Quarter from the Tooth Fairy* avoid confusion when it comes to figuring out all the things he could possibly buy with his quarter. The lessons connect to a variety of gorgeously illustrated and entertaining literature—from the life-size illustrations of coins in the delightful book *Jenny Found a Penny* to the humorous lyrics of Shel Silverstein's beloved poem, "Smart."

The Lessons

Formative Assessment
93

Literature Used in This Chapter

Jenny Found a Penny by Trudy Harris

A Quarter from the Tooth Fairy by Caren Holtzman

The poem *"Smart"* from *Where the Sidewalk Ends* by Shel Silverstein

Additional Idea$ for Parent$

What's a Half-Dollar?

Practice counting on for young learners

Overview

The lessons in Chapter 1 provided opportunities for students to explore pennies, nickels, dimes, and quarters. Since half-dollars aren't used as often as quarters, students may not have been exposed to this coin. This lesson introduces the half-dollar and serves as a springboard for students to further practice the mathematical skills counting on and combinations. It specifically prepares students for the next lesson, 3.2, in which they read the book *Jenny Found a Penny* (and she also finds a half-dollar!).

Common Core State Standards for Mathematics:

Number and Operations in Base Ten   1.NBT.1.2.a.b.c
- *Extend the counting sequence*
- *Understand place value*

Number and Operations in Base Ten   2.NBT.1.a.b.2.7
- *Understand place value*
- *Use place value understanding and properties of operations to add and subtract*

Measurement and Data   2.MD.8
- *Work with time and money*

Mathematics Goals

Students will:
▶ solve word problems involving money
▶ use coin values to add and subtract within fifty
▶ think of ten (dimes) as a bundle of ones

Economics Goals

Students will show:
▶ understanding of the Concept of Money by:
  • recognizing various forms of U.S. currency

Materials

1 quarter and 1 half-dollar for every two to three students

a small collection of pennies, dimes, and nickels for every two to three students

Time

20 minutes

Teaching Directions

Part 1: Introducing the Half-Dollar

1. Gather students in the whole-group area of your classroom. Provide a half-dollar and a quarter for each group of two to three students. Ask students to describe what they see on the half-dollar. Ask them to compare the two coins.

2. Tell students that two half-dollars can be exchanged for a dollar. Explain that a half-dollar is worth fifty cents and then ask the students the key questions.

Part 2: Counting On Using a Half-Dollar

3. Reinforce the idea that half-dollars are worth fifty cents by counting on starting with fifty. Count on from half-dollars, first with a few pennies and then with dimes in a whole group.

4. Explain to students that they are going to build certain amounts of money using a half-dollar. For example, say, "Work with a partner and build fifty-six cents. Build seventy cents. Build fifty-five cents." Do not go above a target amount of one dollar.

5. Place students in partners or small groups. As they work on the activity, circulate, observing, encouraging thinking, and providing support as needed.

Financial Fact

The picture on the half-dollar is of President John Kennedy. He was the youngest president ever elected. The half-dollar has a reeded edge and is larger than a quarter. The reverse of the Kennedy half-dollar is based on the presidential seal.

Key Questions

How many quarters would we need to trade for a half-dollar?

How many dimes would we need to trade for a half-dollar?

How many pennies would we need to trade for a half-dollar?

Teaching Insight: What Coins to Use

For young children, use only half-dollars and pennies. For students who skip count but have difficulties, use half-dollars and either dimes or nickels. Students who count on with fluency should be challenged to build amounts using pennies, nickels, and dimes with one half-dollar.

Extensions

For students who are able to easily count on using combinations of half-dollars, quarters, dimes, nickels, and pennies, increase the target amount to amounts up to five dollars.

Financial Fact

Benjamin Franklin's likeness was shown on half-dollar coins from 1948 to 1975. The reverse of the Franklin half-dollar showed the Liberty Bell. Though Benjamin Franklin was never president of the United States, he was an historic figure and a major force in shaping our country.

Idea$ for Parent$

You can use this lesson at home with your child just as it is written here. Make sure you have a half-dollar coin. Look at it closely with your child. For Part 2 of this lesson, it is appropriate for all children to bump into the idea of counting on from fifty. If your child only counts ones, count on from fifty only with pennies (i.e., fifty, fifty-one, fifty-two…). If your child skip counts by fives and tens, count on from fifty—first by dimes and then by nickels.

For further insights on making purchasing transactions a financial learning opportunity for your child, see the section, Additional Ideas for Parents, page 94. See also the Letter to the Parents, page 233.

Jenny Found a Penny

An economics and math lesson for young learners

Overview

Jenny saves her coins—pennies, nickels, dimes—even a half-dollar—to purchase something special. But there's one thing she forgot to save for. The popular children's book *Jenny Found a Penny* opens the doors for rich mathematical learning and financial understandings in this lesson. Unique to *Jenny Found a Penny* are the book's life-sized illustrations of coins in the sidebars, which help readers add up Jenny's money. The lesson provides page-by-page guidance for using the book to reinforce math concepts in a whole-group setting and to introduce the financial concept of sales tax, concluding with a graphing project that involves every student's voice. It's appropriate for all ability levels.

Common Core State Standards for Mathematics:

Measurement and Data   K.MD.3
  • *Classify objects and count the number of objects in each category*

Number and Operations in Base Ten   1.NBT.2.4
  • *Understand place value*
  • *Use place value understanding and properties of operations to add and subtract*

Measurement and Data   1.MD.4
  • *Represent and interpret data*

Number and Operations in Base Ten   2.NBT.1.a.2.5
  • *Understand place value*
  • *Use place value understanding and properties of operations to add and subtract*

Measurement and Data   2.MD.8.10
  • *Work with time and money*
  • *Represent and interpret data*

Mathematics Goals

Students will:
▶ solve simple compare problems involving information from graphs
▶ count coins
▶ solve problems involving money
▶ use place value understanding to add and subtract
▶ add within one hundred

Economics Goals

Students will show:
▶ understanding of the Concept of Money by:
  • recognizing various forms of U.S. currency
▶ understanding of the concept of Earning Money by:
  • discussing that people make goods and perform services
▶ understanding of the Concept of Wants and Needs by:
  • explaining that individuals and families cannot have everything they want

Time

1 class period

Literature Connections

Jenny Found a Penny by Trudy Harris

Materials

Will Jenny Save Her Money or Spend Her Money? Graph, enlarged for class use (Reproducible 3.2)

1 half-dollar, 1 quarter, 2 dimes, 2 nickels, and 5 pennies, 1 set for each pair of students

Teaching Directions

Part 1: Introducing the Book

1. Gather students in the whole-group area of your classroom. Before you start reading, show students the cover of the book *Jenny Found a Penny.* Ask, "What do you think this book is about?" Give students time to think and then share their predictions.

Part 2: Reading the Book

2. Read the book to students, making sure they can see the illustrations.

3. After you have read the story to students, ask key questions (Set 1).

4. Listen as children tell stories about finding coins.

Teaching Insight:
Picture Books
When reading picture books in whole-group settings, consider using a document camera or some form of technology that will project the illustrations for the whole class to more easily see.

Part 3: Reading the Book: Focusing on Math

5. Start through the book again. Notice the coins at the side of the double-page layout. As you look at each page ask students more key questions (Set 2).

6. Note that on page 8 there are pennies and nickels. Count the money with students.

7. On page 11 a dime has been added. Ask students, "How much is a dime worth?" Count the money with students.

8. On page 13 a quarter is added. Ask students with money-counting experience, "How much money does Jenny have?" Then ask students, "How did you figure that out?"

9. On page 15 a half-dollar appears. Ask students, "How much is a half-dollar worth?" Make sure students hear that a half-dollar is worth fifty cents. Count the money together.

10. Make sure students know Jenny had coins worth a dollar. Discuss that Jenny could have exchanged those coins for a dollar bill.

11. Reread pages 16, 17, and 18—where the dollar store cashier tells Jenny she has a problem. Ask students to tell what her problem was and then ask the key question (Set 3).

Key Questions

Set 1

Has anyone ever found a coin?

What did you do with the coins you found?

In the story Jenny saved the coins she found. Did anyone here save the coins they found?

Key Questions

Set 2

How many coins are there?

How much money is that worth?

Key Question

Set 3

What happens if you want something in a store but you don't have enough money?

12. Ask students to retell what happened next. Turn to page 28 and count the money with students.

Part 4: Understanding Sales Tax

13. Ask if anyone remembers how much sales tax there was (seven cents). Ask students, "How much change should Jenny receive?" Have students explain their thinking.

Part 5: Graphing

14. Have students think about what Jenny bought. Ask them, "What do you think Jenny will do with money she finds or earns in the future?"

15. Show students the graph (see Reproducible 3.2). Ask students to put a mark on the "Save her money" side of the graph if they think Jenny will save the money she finds. Ask students to put a mark on the "Spend her money" side of the graph if they think Jenny will spend the money she finds.

16. When students have finished marking the graph, consider asking key questions.

17. Students may or may not be able to draw conclusions from this information, but it may be a reflection of the choices they make when it comes to spending or saving.

Teaching Insight: Sales Tax
Be prepared to tell students the amount of sales tax charged on each dollar in your state. Explain that many state governments charge a tax on the money people spend on things. In the state of Idaho the sales tax is 6 percent, which means that for every dollar spent six cents is added to the bill. Sales tax varies from state to state and sometimes from city to city within states. Some states, such as Montana, have no sales tax. If you live in a state that has sales tax, ask students, "Is a dollar enough to buy something at the dollar store?"

Key Questions

Which column has the most responses?

Which column has the least responses?

Are there more students who think Jenny will spend her money than save her money?

How many more students think Jenny will spend the money she gets in the future?

Extensions

For another experience with the book *Jenny Found a Penny*, appropriate for students who have had experience counting money, partner students at their tables and give each of them a set of coins that matches Jenny's collection (see Materials list). Ideally use a document camera or a means of enlarging the pages of the book so students can easily see the coins in the margins. Proceed with reading the book, this time stopping and doing the following, encouraging students to add their set of coins to match Jenny's collection.

a. On page 4, read about Jenny finding one penny in the backseat of the car. Ask students to put the same coins on their workspace. Then ask, "How much does Jenny have now? How much more does Jenny need to make a dollar?" When students respond, ask: "How do you know? Did anyone think about it in a different way?"

b. On page 6, Jenny finds four pennies. Again ask, "How much does Jenny have now? How much more does Jenny need to make a dollar? How do you know?"

c. Continue reading the book, asking key questions about each two-page layout.

d. When you reach page 28, ask the key questions again, only instead of the second question, ask: "How much more than a dollar does Jenny have now?"

Key Questions

How much does Jenny have now?

How much more does Jenny need to make a dollar?

How do you know?

Who thought about it in a different way? Explain.

Idea$ for Parent$

Read the book in this lesson at home with your child. Encourage discussions about sales taxes and why we need to account for it when we are making purchases. Use the graphing activity as a discussion starter.

For further insights on making purchasing transactions a financial learning opportunity for your child, see the section, Additional Ideas for Parents, page 94. See also the Letter to the Parents, page 233.

Will Jenny Save Her Money or Spend Her Money? Graph

Save her money	Spend her money

3.3

A Penny Hunt

Practice in counting coins and writing equations for young learners

Overview

Inspired by the book *Jenny Found a Penny* (see Lesson 3.2), students embark on their own classroom hunt for hidden coins in this lesson. The lesson opens with students collecting data on who has found coins before. Once students complete their penny hunt, they use their newfound pennies as counters to work with ten-frames in writing addition and subtraction equations (younger students can simply count coins). Teach this lesson after students have read and are familiar with the book *Jenny Found a Penny* (see Lesson 3.2).

Mathematics Goals

Students will:
▶ count to know how many
▶ compose and decompose numbers
▶ represent addition with pennies on a ten-frame
▶ work with equations
▶ represent and interpret data

Common Core State Standards for Mathematics:

Counting and Cardinality   K.CC.1.2.4.a.b.c.5
- *Know number names and the count sequence*
- *Count to tell the number of objects*

Operations and Algebraic Thinking   1.OA.7
- *Work with addition and subtraction equations*

Measurement and Data   1.MD.4
- *Represent and interpret data*

Literature Connections

Jenny Found a Penny by Trudy Harris

Time

1 class period

Materials

2 pieces of tag board or laminated colored construction paper (can be the same materials used in Lesson 2.1)

clothespins, 1 per student

pennies

playing cards (with numbers)

Ten-Frame sheet (Reproducible 3.3), 1 copy per student

Teaching Insight:
Materials

For very young children, have four to six pennies for each child. For late kindergarten or first-grade students, have six to nine pennies for each child. Use playing cards (with corresponding numbers) or create number cards out of small index cards.

Teaching Directions

Part 1: Preparing the Lesson

1. Prior to this lesson, hide the pennies (see Materials list) around the classroom. Also prepare and display two different colors of tag board or laminated colored construction paper for data collection (you can use the same materials you used for data collection in Lesson 2.1).

Part 2: Introducing the Lesson: Collecting Data

2. Tell students, "We are going to do some quick data collection." Use sticky notes to indicate which piece of tag board is "yes" and which is "no" or other responses. Give each student a clothespin; explain to students that they will be answering questions by clipping their clothespin to the tag board that matches their response.

3. Remind students of the book *Jenny Found a Penny* (see Lesson 3.2). Ask students, "Have you ever found a coin?" Give students time to clip their clothespins to either the "yes" or the "no" tag board.

4. After the collection of data, ask the key questions.

Key Questions

What do you notice about our data?

What would someone coming into our classroom know about us when they see our data?

Which had the most responses?

Which had the least responses?

How many more/less were there?

Part 3: Hunting for Pennies

5. Explain to students that you have hidden pennies around the room. You are going to have students draw a card. They need to search until they have found the number of pennies that is equal to the number on their card. When they have found their pennies, they should return to their workspace.

Part 4: Using Ten-Frames

6. While students are searching for pennies, put a ten-frame sheet (Reproducible 3.3) at each student's workspace. When all students have returned to their tables, ask them to put their pennies on their ten-frames.

7. Model placing pennies on a ten-frame; use a student's work as an example (e.g., if a student put three on each row, put yours in the same arrangement). At this stage, for preK students, simply ask them to count their coins. For kindergarten and first-grade students, model writing equations that match their arrangements. For example, for the student who has three pennies on

> **Teaching Insight:**
> **Using Ten-Frames**
> If this is the first time using ten-frames in your class, begin by asking students, "How many spaces are on the ten-frame?" Turn the ten-frame vertically and ask, "How many spaces are on the ten-frame now?" Help students understand that the number of spaces on the ten-frame is ten regardless of whether it is horizontal or vertical.

each row, write *3 + 3 = 6*. If another student's ten-frame has three pennies in the first row and four in the second row, write *3 + 4 = 7*.

8. Once students are familiar with the task, ask them to record on the ten-frame and write their equation below it.

Part 5: Processing the Experience

9. In a whole-group setting, ask students who found six pennies to bring their ten-frame papers to the front of the class. Display the papers in a group for everyone to see. Then ask students who found seven pennies to bring their papers to the front. Display the papers in a group for everyone to see. Continue until all papers are displayed.

10. Now look at the group of papers corresponding to six pennies. Record the different equations together on a list for everyone to see. Ask students, "Are there any other ways to make six that we didn't find?" Give students time to find missing equations. Write those equations. Do the same for the other numbers.

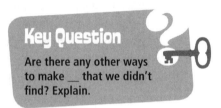

Key Question

Are there any other ways to make ___ that we didn't find? Explain.

Extensions

For students with more experience in writing equations, extend the task by asking them to record an equation in answer to the question, "How many more to make ten?" For example, a student with six pennies could write *6 + 4 = 10* or *10 − 6 = 4*.

Ideas for Parents

Read the book in this lesson at home with your child. For the data collection part (Part 1), simply ask your child to recall an experience he or she may have had finding a coin. Then go ahead—have a penny hunt in your home! Work with your child using the ten-frame reproducible. Vary the number of pennies hidden and repeat this lesson to build different combinations of numbers.

For further insights on making purchasing transactions a financial learning opportunity for your child, see the section, Additional Ideas for Parents, page 94. See also the Letter to the Parents, page 233.

Ten-Frame

Name: _____

My Equations:

Quarter from the Tooth Fairy

Practice in combinations and constructing equivalent equations

Overview

In *A Quarter from the Tooth Fairy,* part of the Scholastic Math Readers collection, a young boy adds up all the different things he can buy for twenty-five cents and gets so confused that he decides to buy his tooth back. This humorous tale launches students into the task of creating as many combinations as they can to make twenty-five cents. Students record their thinking and reconvene as a whole group to construct equivalent equations.

Common Core State Standards for Mathematics:

Operations and Algebraic Thinking   1.OA.1.2.3.7
- *Represent and solve problems involving addition and subtraction*
- *Understand and apply properties of operations and the relationship between addition and subtraction*
- *Work with addition and subtraction equations*

Operations and Algebraic Thinking   2.OA.1
- *Represent and solve problems involving addition and subtraction*

Number and Operations in Base Ten   2.NBT.2
- *Understand place value*

Measurement and Data   2.MD.8
- *Work with time and money*

Mathematics Goals

Students will:
- ▶ use addition to solve problems
- ▶ work with addition equations
- ▶ solve problems using money
- ▶ find combinations that equal twenty-five

Time

1 class period

Materials

paper

25 pennies, 6 nickels, and 3 dimes for each student

Literature Connections

A Quarter from the Tooth Fairy by Caren Holtzman

Teaching Directions

Part 1: Reading the Book

1. Gather students in the whole-group area of your classroom. Read the book *A Quarter from the Tooth Fairy*. The first time through, just read and enjoy the book.

2. Have students retell the trading of coins.

Part 2: Recording Ways to Show Twenty-Five Cents

3. Give each student a plain sheet of paper and a set of coins (see Materials list). Ask students to find all the possible ways to show twenty-five cents and to record the ways they find. Have students work individually or with a partner. Let them know that more paper is available if they need it to finish recording.

4. Circulate as students are working. Note those students who recorded only one or two ways to make twenty-five cents but seem to be finished. Ask those students to explain how they know they found all the ways.

Part 3: Constructing Equivalent Equations

5. When students are finished, reconvene as a whole group. Ask students to describe the combinations they found. Record students' thinking for everyone in the class to see.

6. Use the information students give you to construct equivalent equations. For example, if a student says twenty-five cents can be made using only nickels, write the problem: $5 + 5 + 5 + 5 + 5 = 25$. The next student might say she used two dimes and one nickel. Write the equation: $10 + 10 + 5 = 25$. Then write $5 + 5 + 5 + 5 + 5 = 10 + 10 + 5$ and ask students if the equation is correct. Ask students to explain how they know. Use a few more equivalent equations as students describe different ways to build twenty-five cents.

> **Teaching Insight:**
> **Equivalent Equations**
> Equivalent means the same. Equations are considered to be equivalent if they have the same solution. For example: $5 + 5 + 5 + 5 + 5 = 25$ and $10 + 10 + 5 = 25$; therefore, the two equations can be said to be equivalent and $5 + 5 + 5 + 5 + 5 = 10 + 10 + 5$.

7. For some first-grade and all second-grade students, ask students to write their own equivalent equations showing different ways to reach twenty-five. Continue sharing ways to reach twenty-five.

Teaching Insight:
Combinations of Twenty-Five
The following table shows all the possible ways to make twenty-five cents with pennies, nickels, dimes, and a quarter. Young children will draw their solutions to the problem of how many ways to make twenty-five cents. Some second-grade students may begin to chart options instead of drawing coins, especially if they have had experience with T-charts.

Quarters	Dimes	Nickels	Pennies		Total Amount
1	0	0	0		25
0	2	1	0		25
0	2	0	5		25
0	1	3	0		25
0	1	2	5		25
0	1	1	10		25
0	1	0	15		25
0	0	2	15		25
0	0	3	10		25
0	0	4	5		25
0	0	5	0		25
0	0	1	20		25
0	0	0	25		25

Idea$ for Parent$

You can use this lesson at home with your child just as it is written here. Read the book in this lesson to your child. If your child is not skip counting, he or she will enjoy this book but will need assistance in building combinations. Model writing these equations for your child without expecting her or him to write.

For further insights on making purchasing transactions a financial learning opportunity for your child, see the section, Additional Ideas for Parents, page 94. See also the Letter to the Parents, page 233.

Being "Smart" About Trading Money

A lesson in the value of coins for young learners

Overview

"Smart" is a poem about a boy whose dad gives him a dollar bill. Feeling smart, the boy trades the dollar bill for two quarters—after all, two is better than one! He then trades the two quarters for three dimes—and continues thinking he's increasingly smart, letting the quantity of coins, rather than the value of coins, determine his trades. What happens when he returns to his father with five pennies instead of the one-dollar bill? Shel Silverstein's poems have been loved by students for many years, and this one is no exception. Offering a humorous take on the value of money, the poem launches students into a task of correcting the boy's thinking—and surfacing smarter ways to trade money. This lesson is appropriate for all ability levels.

Mathematics Goals

Students will:
▶ add and subtract
▶ solve problems using money

Common Core State Standards for Mathematics:

Operations and Algebraic Thinking   1.OA.1
- *Represent and solve problems involving addition and subtraction*

Number and Operations in Base Ten   2.NBT.2
- *Understand place value*

Measurement and Data   2.MD.8
- *Work with time and money*

Economics Goals

Students will show:
▶ understanding of the Concept of Money by:
  • recognizing various forms of U.S. currency

Materials

paper and pencil for each student

Time

1 class period

Literature Connections

The poem "Smart" from *Where the Sidewalk Ends* by Shel Silverstein

Teaching Directions

Part 1: Reading the Poem

1. Gather students in the whole-group area of your classroom. Read the poem "Smart" from *Where the Sidewalk Ends*.

2. Retell the poem using the illustrations and coins. Start with a dollar bill. Ask students, "What was wrong when the son traded the dollar bill for two quarters?" Have students explain their thinking. Ask, "How many quarters should the son have received if he made a trade that was equivalent to the dollar bill?" As you continue through the poem, ask questions and record each trade made in a list where everyone can see it (see Figure 3–1).

Money he had	Coins he received
1 dollar	2 quarters
2 quarters	3 dimes
3 dimes	4 nickels
4 nickels	5 pennies

Figure 3–1. The Trades Made in the Poem "Smart"

Part 2: Making Trades

3. Ask students to work with a partner. Using words and pictures, they need to show at least one trade that should have been made instead of the trade the boy made. For example, students could show that the two quarters really should have been traded for five dimes.

4. While students are working, circulate, observing their work, noting if their thinking is correct, and answering any questions.

Part 3: Processing the Experience

5. When students have finished writing, gather them to discuss their thinking in a whole-group setting. Go through the trades made and ask students to read what they wrote.

Idea$ for Parent$

Read the poem in this lesson to your child. Encourage a discussion about why the trades in the poem aren't fair trades. Have your child show in words and pictures a trade that should have been made. Encourage your child to explain his or her thinking.

For further insights on making purchasing transactions a financial learning opportunity for your child, see the section, Additional Ideas for Parents, page 94. See also the Letter to the Parents, page 233.

Getting Change Back
A problem-solving approach for young learners

Overview

In this lesson, money provides the context for students to solve one- and two-step word problems on a daily basis. When students are first introduced to this lesson, take time to discuss the various meanings of the word *change*, focusing on what it means to make change when using money. In the problem-solving procedure that ensues the discussion is much the same for students counting one penny at a time versus students who are using number relationships and a variety of strategies to solve problems. Use only one question a day, planning to take five to fifteen minutes for the whole process. Use what you learn during this time to plan for instruction if misconceptions or lack of proficiency are evident.

Common Core State Standards for Mathematics:

Counting and Cardinality   K.CC.1.2.4.5
- *Know number names and the count sequence*
- *Count to tell the number of objects*

Operations and Algebraic Thinking   1.OA.1.2.4.5.6.7.8
- *Represent and solve problems involving addition and subtraction*
- *Understand and apply properties of operations and the relationship between addition and subtraction*
- *Add and subtract within 20*
- *Work with addition and subtraction equations*

Number and Operations in Base Ten   1.NBT.2.a.b.c.3.4.5.6
- *Understand place value*
- *Use place value understanding and properties of operations to add and subtract*

Operations and Algebraic Thinking   2.OA.1
- *Represent and solve problems involving addition and subtraction*

Number and Operations in Base Ten   2.NBT.1.a.2.5.6.8
- *Understand place value*
- *Use place value understanding and properties of operations to add and subtract*

Measurement and Data 2.MD.8
- *Work with time and money*

Mathematics Goals

Students will:
- ▶ represent addition and subtraction
- ▶ solve addition and subtraction word problems
- ▶ think of two-digit numbers as tens and ones
- ▶ use knowledge of tens and ones in addition and subtraction problems
- ▶ solve problems involving money

Materials

a daily problem from the appropriate List 3.6A, 3.6B, 3.6C, or 3.6D

chart paper or some means of displaying written lists for students to see

Time

5 to 15 minutes per problem

Teaching Directions

Part 1: Exploring the Word *Change*

1. Gather students in the whole-group area of your classroom. Tell them that you are going to talk about the word *change*. The word *change* has many meanings, many of which are used daily. Ask students to volunteer some of their understandings of the word *change*. Teach and/or clarify meanings as necessary.

Teaching Insight: The Word *Change*
The word *change* has several meanings:
- change can be a verb, as in *change a light bulb*
- change, also as a verb, can mean to modify, as in *to change your mind*
- change can also mean to switch or trade, as in *change places* or *change seats*
- change can mean to abandon, as in *change sides*
- change can mean to exchange, as in *If you like my toy, I will change with you*
- change can mean *to put on other clothing*
- change can mean a transition from one phase to another, as in *a change of seasons*
- change can mean to cause something to be different, as in *change the spelling of a word*
- change can mean to transfer from one to another, as in *change planes in another city*
- change, as a noun, can refer to *the change, or coins carried in a pocket*
- change can also mean the balance of money returned at the end of a transaction, as in *getting change back from your dollar*
- change can also be the exchange of smaller denomination money for money of higher denominations, as in *Can you change this dollar so I'll have some quarters?*

2. Explain that knowing how to give or receive change from a larger amount of money is important. If you don't know how to give or receive change, you will never be sure that you received the right amount of money. The person giving you change may have made an error and you would never know.

Teaching Insight: The Word *Change*
Making change (giving a balance of money returned after a transaction or exchanging smaller denominations for larger money denominations) is a challenging task for even some adults. In stores, computerized cash registers tell cashiers how much change to give. Before we had that type of cash register, people had to count change themselves. There is a counting backward procedure that people who count change use. For the purpose of this lesson, do not teach that procedure. Making sense of amounts is more important than being able to follow a procedure in determining the amount of money returned after a purchase or in exchanging coins for smaller denomination coins. Asking students to think about the money returned helps them build number sense. They can learn the common procedure for counting change when they are more fluent with composing and decomposing numbers. Before students are fluent with building numbers, following this procedure would just be a memorized task.

Part 2: Solving Problems

3. Once students are comfortable with the word *change* as it applies to money, explain to them that they will be solving a daily problem about counting money and making change. Adhere to the following same procedure each day, using a different problem—but only one—each day. Choose problems that are appropriate for your students' abilities from Lists 3.6A, 3.6B, 3.6C, and 3.6D.

4. During the daily problem-solving process do not provide direction or give students a procedure for solving the problem. Create a safe environment by making students comfortable sharing answers even when they are different from other students' answers. Facilitate by asking key questions.

Daily Problem-Solving Procedure

1. Prepare a place to record student responses where everyone can see them (consider using chart paper or the board).
2. Select and present a problem for students to solve (see Lists 3.6A, 3.6B, 3.6C, and 3.6D on pages 89–92).
3. Give students time to find an answer (this should be a mental task).
4. Have students share their answers. Encourage students to explain their thinking.
5. Record student responses and the strategies they used to find their answers.

Key Questions

How did you figure it out?

Did anyone think about it in a different way?

Who else did the problem Sarah's way?

Why did you do that?

Can you tell me what you were thinking?

What strategies do you see used?

Which strategies seem to be simpler?

Who did it another way?

Does anyone have any questions for Sarah?

Who started the problem this same way?

What did you do next?

Teaching Insight: Supporting Students in Describing Strategies

Ask questions regardless of whether a wrong or a right answer is given so students don't assume that if you're asking a question, their strategy must be wrong. When you record student responses, label them as "Sarah's Way" or by strategy such as "Using Doubles."

When students describe a strategy without naming it, restate the strategy used and name it. For example, "I see you counted on from __ to solve this problem," or "I see that your strategy was making a ten." If possible, connect to strategies students already use. Students describe the ways they added to, took from, took apart, or put together numbers. Students should begin to use strategies such as using landmark numbers or doubles to find answers.

For example, tell your students that you went to the store to buy something. It cost eighty-six cents. You gave the clerk one dollar. How much change should you have received? Where everyone can see it, write *$1.00 paid*. Then write *86* with a cents sign or with a decimal, depending on your students' previous experience with decimals. Record the strategies used. Expect some students to count on from eighty-six to one hundred. Some students might count from eighty-six to ninety and then add ten. Students might subtract ten from one hundred and count backward from ninety to eighty-six. Listen to students as they suggest ways to solve the problem. Record their strategies.

When students have agreed on an answer, ask, "Why is it important to know how much change you are getting? How many different ways could the clerk have given the fourteen cents in change?" (one dime and four pennies, two nickels and four pennies, one nickel and nine pennies, or fourteen pennies).

Idea$ for Parent$

You can use this lesson at home with your child just as it is written here. Since a variety of responses can't happen when working with only one child, ask, "Is there another way we could think about it? Can you find another way to solve this problem?" Set aside time on a daily basis to do one of the problems with your child.

For further insights on making purchasing transactions a financial learning opportunity for your child, see the section, Additional Ideas for Parents, page 94. See also the Letter to the Parents, page 233.

Making Change: Daily Problems

PreK–K

Making change can be a challenging task for children. For prekindergarten and kindergarten students, counting by ones makes sense. Children at this age also begin counting objects in combined sets and counting objects in sets with objects removed. Prekindergarten students should act out situations and make sense of the problems. Kindergarten students should start to follow the routine procedure in solving the problem. Problems to use with prekindergarten and kindergarten students:

- I bought two things at the store. One cost three cents. The other cost two cents. How much did I spend?
- If I had seven cents and the store clerk gave me three cents, how much money would I have altogether?
- If I had ten cents and the store clerk gave me five cents, how much money would I have altogether?
- I bought two things at the store. One cost eight cents. The other cost two cents. How much did I spend?
- I had ten cents. I spent four cents. How much did I have left?
- I had five cents. I spent four cents. How much did I have left?
- I bought something at the store. It cost five cents. I paid with a dime, which is worth ten cents. How much change should I get?

Making Change: Daily Problems

First Grade

First-grade students start using information about the value of coins. They develop strategies for adding and subtracting whole numbers and start using what they know about relationships with numbers to solve problems. Problems to use with first-grade students:

- I went to the store and bought something that cost fourteen cents. I gave the clerk twenty cents. How much change should I have received?
- I bought two things at the store. One cost seventeen cents. The other cost twelve cents. Can I pay for this with a quarter?
- I had fifty cents. I spent forty cents. How much money did I have left?
- I gave the clerk a dollar and he gave me back ten cents. How much did I spend?
- I received ten cents back when I gave the clerk a quarter. How much did I spend?
- I bought something for twenty-five cents. I gave the clerk three nickels and one dime. Would I get any change back?
- I bought two things. One cost fifty cents. The other cost twenty cents. How much change would I get back from a dollar?

Making Change: Daily Problems

Second Grade

Second-grade students need to work on fluency adding and subtracting numbers up to one hundred. Their ability to count on and count back by ones and tens makes counting change from a dollar accessible for them. Problems to use with second-grade students:

- I bought something for seventy-three cents. I gave the clerk three quarters. Was that enough money?
- I bought something for fifteen cents. I gave the clerk a dollar. I got back three quarters. Was my change correct?
- I need to give thirty-seven cents change. What combination of coins is the fewest possible?
- Luke has some pennies and some dimes. He has five coins. How much money could Luke have?
- I bought something for forty-seven cents and something else for fifty-two cents. Is a dollar enough to purchase these items?
- I found gum on sale for twenty-five cents each. I bought three of them. How much change would I receive from one dollar?
- My friend borrowed a dollar from me. He gave me a candy bar worth fifty cents, two dimes, one nickel, and three pennies. Does he still owe me money? If so, how much money does he owe?
- Explain that you went to the store and bought something. You gave the clerk a dollar. She gave you twenty-six cents change. How much did you spend?
- I bought a present for my friend that cost seventy cents. If the change from a dollar was made with dimes, how many dimes would I get back?

Making Change: Daily Problems

Third, Fourth, and Fifth Grades

Students who are proficient money counters in the grades following second grade are asked to make change up to five dollars. Some first- and many second-grade students may be ready to move beyond their grade level expectations. The following problems may be used in classrooms where students are proficient at counting coins and are ready to think in terms of larger amounts of money.

- I want to buy two things at the store. One costs one dollar and fifty cents and the other costs three dollars. I have five dollars. Do I have enough money to pay for these things?
- I received three dollars and fifty cents in change. I gave the clerk five dollars. How much did I spend?
- I found a toy that costs one dollar and fifty cents. I have five dollars. How many toys can I buy?
- I bought something for four dollars. I gave the clerk five dollars. The clerk gave me two quarters, three dimes, and four nickels. Did I get the right change?
- I had four dollars. I spent one dollar and fifty cents. How much did I have left?
- I bought something for seventy-five cents. I gave the clerk a five-dollar bill. What coins and bills should I get back?
- I want to buy some gum for one dollar and twenty-five cents and candy for one dollar and seventy-five cents. I have three dollars. Is that enough money?

CHAPTER 3
Do We Have Enough Money?

Formative Assessment

While students are working on the problems posed in this chapter's lessons, you may want to make the following observations:

- How did children describe how they solved the problem?
- Did students have confidence in solving these problems?
- Did students work cooperatively?
- Did students who drew to solve problems find an efficient way to illustrate or did they draw in great detail?
- How firm were students in their beliefs when questioned?
- Did students use math language, such as "plus" and "minus"?
- Did students draw or use numbers or symbols to represent the different ways to make twenty-five?
- Were students able to write equations based on coin combinations that totaled twenty-five?
- How did students count coins? Did they start with the largest coin in the group, make a ten, or were they inconsistent?
- Did students use landmark numbers or friendlier numbers to determine how much?
- Were any students quickly bored with an activity? If so, this could indicate a need for more challenge; students could be pushed further in future tasks.

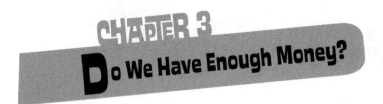

Additional Idea$ for Parent$

Helping Your Child Be Financially Savvy with Purchasing Transactions

A big idea of this chapter is knowing whether you have enough money to buy something you want. When children watch their parents make purchases, they usually do not have access to this decision-making process. You are likely mentally figuring out whether you can afford what you are buying, but your child just sees you make the purchase. It's not necessarily a good idea to share your own financial situation with your child, but it is a good idea to talk with your child about purchases she or he makes with her or his allowance—and carry through with the transaction, helping your child count her or his money to see if there is enough (see the Additional Ideas for Parents section in Chapter 2, page 61, for guidance on using an allowance as a financial learning opportunity).

Sometimes our first instinct is to take over the purchasing transaction for the item the child wants—it's often quicker, but not financially savvy. Rather, think about the financial knowledge your child could acquire in such opportunities. Take a moment to walk through the purchasing transaction with your child. Say, "That item costs ___. Let's count your money and see if you have enough to pay for it." Instead of saying, "You can't afford that!" say, "Have you saved enough money for it yet?" If it is something your child really wants but has no urgent reason to buy, say something like, "It looks as though it doesn't fit your budget this month, but you can save your allowance and buy it next month." Follow up by helping your child create a financial plan on paper; he or she can figure out how much of his or her allowance needs to be saved and add the next allowance to the total until your child can afford what is wanted.

Sometimes when confronted with the problem of not being able to buy something because it is too expensive, your child will choose not to save up for that item but to buy a less expensive alternative. Consider this a learning experience. As adults, when we can't afford what we really want, we often choose a less expensive alternative.

See also the Letter to the Parents, page 233.

My Reflections, Lesson Notes, and Ideas

CHAPTER 4

Why Can't We Have Everything?

**Explore the Differences Between Needs and Wants—From Survival Lists
and Bartering to the Consequences of Unplanned Overspending**

Overview

This chapter addresses the differences between needs and wants. Students have an opportunity to think further about why we can't have everything and the consequences when we spend without thinking.

Lesson 4.1 introduces students to the beautiful multicultural book *All Kinds of Children*, helping children see and understand that midst their many differences, there are many similarities—one of them being that all children have the same needs.

Lesson 4.2 deepens students' understanding of wants versus needs, putting students in charge of planning a survival needs list for a pretend adventure trip.

In **Lesson 4.3** students counsel Alexander in his story, *Alexander, Who Used to Be Rich Last Sunday*. The lesson provides opportunities to count money and to respond to Alexander's problem of unplanned spending. The idea of bartering is revisited in **Lesson 4.4** through the flavorful Latin American story *Saturday Sancocho*.

Lessons 4.5 and **4.6** continue to build on students' mathematical and financial skills. Students collect data, build graphs, instantly recognize numbers, and compare the value of coins in a quick-paced game of *Grab and Go!*

The Lessons

Formative Assessment
124

Literature Used in This Chapter

All Kinds of Children by Norma Simon

Alexander, Who Used to Be Rich Last Sunday by Judith Viorst

Saturday Sancocho by Leyla Torres

Additional Idea$ for Parent$

Do You Want It or Do You Need It?

An economics lesson for young learners

Overview

This lesson opens with a whole-group reading of the beautiful multicultural children's book, *All Kinds of Children.* Applicable to all ages of children, the book explores the lives of children across the world, helping children see and understand that midst their many differences, there are many similarities—one of them being that all children have the same needs, primarily food, clothing, shelter, and people who love them. After reading the book, children create a list of "Wants and Needs." They then think about what's on the list that would also belong on a "Survival Needs" list. Finally students think about which list of items they'd spend their money on first. The lesson supports children in thinking about the differences between "want" and "need," using such criteria to help inform the decisions they make when it comes to spending and saving their money, and ultimately understanding why they can't have everything.

Economics Goals

Students will show:
▶ understanding of the Concept of Wants and Needs by:
- identifying basic human needs
- explaining how basic human needs can be met
- describing the needs of a family
- explaining that individuals and families cannot have everything they want
- identifying examples of wanting more than we have
- explaining why wanting more than we have requires people to make choices

Materials

chart paper or some means of displaying written lists for students to see

Literature Connections

All Kinds of Children by Norma Simon

Time

1 class period

Teaching Directions

Part 1: Reading the Book

1. Gather students in the whole-group area of your classroom. Ask students to turn to a partner. Tell students you are going to give them thirty seconds to think about how they and their partner are alike. Ask students to talk with their partner to share how they thought they were alike. Have students share their thinking about this. You will probably get answers that include, "We are both boys (or girls) . . . we both have eyes . . . we both have mouths . . . we both have curly hair (or straight hair)."

2. Read the book *All Kinds of Children* to students, making sure that they can see the illustrations.

> **Teaching Insight:**
> **Picture Books**
> When reading picture books in whole-group settings, consider using a document camera or some form of technology that will project the illustrations for the whole class to more easily see.

Part 2: Discussing Wants and Needs

3. After reading the book, ask students, "How are children the same? Tell me some ways that you thought of after we read the book." Still expect students to describe physical attributes—they may say such things as "All children have bellybuttons because that's in the book." Listen and talk about the physical attributes children have in common with others across the world. Ask them to think for a moment about how they are alike in some way that we can't see. Give students time to tell what they are thinking.

4. Next, tell students that children everywhere need and want some of the same things. Start a list for everyone to see; label it with the heading *Wants and Needs* at the top. Ask students, "What are wants and needs that all children in all cultures have?" Write the wants and needs down as children tell them to you. Make sure you have food, shelter, and clothing on your list. Include things that are either wants or needs, without labeling or commenting. Continue until the space for your list is almost full.

5. Ask students, "Do you get everything you want when you go to the store?" Facilitate a conversation about things children get and don't get.

6. Start another list where everyone can see it. Label this list with the heading *Survival Needs*. Look at the first list and comment on the amount of things listed. Ask students, "Do you need everything on the *Wants and Needs* list in order to survive?" Consider items one at a time. If the class agrees something is needed to survive, circle it. When things have been circled, ask students, "Is this all that is needed to survive?" Make sure food, shelter, and clothing are circled.

7. Write the circled items on the list labeled *Survival Needs*. If students suggest things that are not needed for survival, question them. Ask, "Can you live without that item?"

Part 3: Making Decisions

8. Next explain to students that when you earn money you have to make decisions about things to buy. Ask students, "If your money is limited, should you spend it on things listed on the *Survival Needs* list or on the *Needs and Wants* list?" Listen to their responses.

9. Then ask students, "If you have money left after you pay for things you need to survive, what can you do with your money?" Listen to students describe things they would buy.

10. Finally, ask students, "If you don't have enough money to buy something you really want, what could you do?" Hopefully some children in the class will suggest saving until you have enough money to buy what you want!

Key Questions

How are children all the same?

What are wants and needs that all children in all cultures have?

Do you get everything you want when you go to the store? Why or why not?

Do you need everything on the *Wants and Needs* list in order to survive? Why or why not?

Is this all that is needed to survive? What's missing?

Can you live without that item? Why or why not?

If your money is limited, should you spend it on things listed on the *Survival Needs* list or on the *Needs and Wants* list? Why or why not?

If you have money left after you pay for things you need to survive, what can you do with your money?

If you don't have enough money to buy something you really want, what could you do?

Financial Facts

Economics is a social science about how people use resources. Our resources can mean our talents, land, buildings, services, equipment, knowledge, materials, and much more. Economists study the use of labor, land, money, income, investments, and government expenditures and taxes.

Economists study decisions that affect trade, production, and consumption, such as marketplaces. Economists look at the well-being of rich people and poor people and try to learn about how people acquire wealth.

Economists consider a *want* to be something that is desired. Usually, economists don't consider wants and needs separately. Instead of considering *wants* and *needs*, economists say that there is just *wants* with various levels of importance.

For the purposes of young children learning about economics ideas, there is a distinction between wants and needs. In terms of needs that must be met for survival, we all have a biological requirement for air, water, food, shelter, and sleep. These contrast with those things we want but are able to survive without. We need food to survive. We want to eat cookies, though we don't need cookies to survive.

People have limited resources and have to make choices to satisfy needs and wants. One big economical idea is that no one gets to have everything they want and everyone has to look for affordable alternatives in satisfying their needs and wants.

Extensions

The book *All Kinds of Children* includes questions for the reader to answer and provide input on throughout the story. Leave this book out so it is available for students to reread, answer the questions, and notice the interesting details in the dynamic illustrations.

Idea$ for Parent$

You can use this lesson at home with your child just as it is written here. Read the book in this lesson at home with your child. Encourage discussions about needs versus wants. Revisit the lesson whenever there is a need to define wants and needs. Extend the lesson into your family life by asking your child as you shop, "Is this a want or a need?"

For further insights on helping your child understand that once money is spent, it's gone, see the section, Additional Ideas for Parents, page 125. See also the Letter to the Parents, page 234.

What Do You Need to Survive?

A survival needs lesson for young learners

Overview

In this lesson students gain a deeper understanding of wants and needs by taking on the role of planners for an adventure trip. Whether the pretend adventure trip be camping in the wilderness or setting out to sea on a sailboat, it's of utmost importance that students know what they'll need to take to survive. What can they leave behind? Working in partners, students create a list of wants and needs, then convene as a whole group to discuss their options.

Economics Goals

Students will show:
▶ understanding of the Concept of Wants and Needs by:
  • identifying basic human needs

Materials

poster-sized paper (newsprint, butcher paper, or 17-by-11-inch copy paper), 1 for each pair or small group of students

Time

1 class period

Teaching Directions

1. Tell students that they are going to pretend they are preparing for a camping trip in the wilderness. Explain that they don't need to be worried about who will take care of them, because there will be adults on their trip. It is their job as children, however, to help plan what to take on this wilderness adventure.

2. Have students first work individually in creating a list of what they'll need for the adventure. Then have them share their work with a partner.

3. Give each group or pair of students a poster-sized sheet of paper. Have students work together to make a "needs and wants" chart of the things they want to bring on a pretend adventure. Ask students, "What will you need to survive?"

4. In a whole-group setting, give students an opportunity to explain what they included as needs and wants on their charts. Make sure that at the end they have thought about shelter, food, water, and clothing. Be prepared to have discussions about some things beyond those basics.

Ideas for Parents

Very young children may find it difficult to pretend they are planning for a survival trip if they have never spent the night in a camping situation. Expand this idea to fit your family habits. When you have a family trip, give your child an opportunity to plan with you and make lists of things you need and want to take.

For further insights on helping your child understand that once money is spent, it's gone, see the section, Additional Ideas for Parents, page 125. See also the Letter to the Parents, page 234.

Teaching Insight:
The Adventure
If your students live somewhere in which a wilderness adventure is unfamiliar to them and hence a challenge to pretending, change the setting to something more familiar, perhaps a beach or a sailboat trip. Make sure the setting makes sense to your students.

Teaching Insight:
Varying the Task
For young children, plan as a whole group; as the teacher, record students' thoughts for everyone to see. First-grade students should be able to complete the task with partners. Part of their instruction should be to include pictures and words to show what they need to take with them on the adventure. Second-grade students should be able to construct lists of things to take on the adventure. Drawings are acceptable but should be accompanied by a written list.

Teaching Insight:
More Wants Than Needs
It is probable that in a whole-group discussion there will be more wants than needs expressed. This is a good time to explain that we all have more wants than needs and we all have to make choices. If we fulfill our wants before we fulfill our needs, we may have problems. Tell students that people everywhere have to make choices like this all the time; very few people are able to have everything they want!

Alexander Used to Be Rich

A lesson in understanding the consequences of unplanned spending for young learners

Overview

This lesson is appropriate for children who recognize coins and have been introduced to coin values. Follow the instructions in the lesson that allow different levels of ability to participate. Many children can relate to Alexander's quandary in the book *Alexander, Who Used to Be Rich Last Sunday.* Feeling rich after just receiving money for his allowance, Alexander somehow spends all he has within a short amount of time, leaving him with only bus tokens. After reading the book, students take on the task of keeping track of Alexander's money. Using addition and subtraction skills, students track Alexander's coins as they hear the story again—until Alexander has no coins left. Students then think about ways to help Alexander make financially smart decisions in the future; they may write a letter to Alexander or draw pictures representing their advice to him. The problem-solving context of this lesson makes it rich both mathematically and financially—albeit Alexander is now poor!

Mathematics Goals

Students will:
▶ use addition and subtraction to solve problems
▶ skip count
▶ solve word problems involving money

Economics Goals

Students will show:
▶ understanding of the Concept of Wants and Needs by:
  • explaining that individuals and families cannot have everything they want
  • identifying examples of wanting more than we have
  • explaining why wanting more than we have requires people to make choices

Common Core State Standards for Mathematics:

Operations and Algebraic Thinking   1.OA.1
  • *Represent and solve problems involving addition and subtraction*

Operations and Algebraic Thinking   2.OA.1
  • *Represent and solve problems involving addition and subtraction*

Number and Operations in Base Ten   2.NBT.2
  • *Understand place value*

Measurement and Data   2.MD.8
  • *Work with time and money*

Literature Connections

Alexander, Who Used to Be Rich Last Sunday by Judith Viorst

Time

1 class period

Materials

7 dimes, 4 nickels, and 10 pennies per student
Alexander's Money (Reproducible 4.3a), 1 copy per student
A Letter to Alexander (Reproducible 4.3b), 1 copy per student

Teaching Directions

Part 1: Reading the Book

1. Gather students in the whole-group area of your classroom. Read the book *Alexander, Who Used to Be Rich Last Sunday* to students, making sure they can see the illustrations.

2. After reading Alexander's story, ask students, "What happened to Alexander's money?" Listen while students retell what happened to Alexander's money. Ask the key questions.

Part 2: Counting Alexander's Money

3. Explain to students that they are now going to keep track of Alexander's money with him. Give one copy of the recording sheet *Alexander's Money* (Reproducible 4.3a) and a set of coins to each student. Have students count their set of coins to make sure they each have seven dimes, four nickels, and ten pennies.

4. Ask students to place the coins in the appropriate places on the graph on their recording sheet. If you are working with young children, you may have to review coin values.

5. Ask students to complete the statements at the top of the graph.

6. Once all students have their coins on their graphs and have completed the statements, reread the book. As you come to each amount Alexander used, give students time to remove the corresponding number of coins from their graphs. Instruct students to put the coins they remove back into the bags. Each time, stop and recount the coins with students. Ask students, "How much money is left?"

7. Continue reading the story, repeating Step 6 until students' graphs no longer have any coins.

8. Ask students to now count the coins in their bags. Does the number match the number on the list in the bag? Collect all coin sets.

Teaching Insight:
Picture Books
When reading picture books in whole-group settings, consider using a document camera or some form of technology that will project the illustrations for the whole class to more easily see.

Teaching Insight:
Sets of Coins
Put each set of coins in plastic sandwich bags ahead of time. Include a note in each bag that lists the number of coins that should be in it. Have students count the coins against the list before returning each bag to you at the end of the lesson.

Key Questions

Did Alexander plan ahead for spending his money?

Did he want to save any money? What did he want to save for?

Do you think Alexander will ever save enough money to buy what he wants?

If you could give Alexander advice, what would it be?

What should Alexander's parents do?

Part 3: Writing a Letter to Alexander

9. Ask students, "Does Alexander need help?" The consensus should be "yes!" Explain to students that one way to help Alexander might be to write a letter of advice to him. They should advise Alexander on what he needs to do when he gets money. Give each student a copy of *A Letter to Alexander* (Reproducible 4.3b). Students who are not able to write should draw what Alexander should do.

10. Circulate as students are writing their letters, prompting their thinking as needed and making notes about any particular challenges.

Extensions

As an extension to this lesson, mail the letters to the book's author, Judith Viorst, via the book's publisher. Encouraging the mailing of lots of letters to Judith Viorst might be overwhelming. Consider instead forwarding a small sample of particularly great letters in hopes that Judith writes back (note that Judith is now in her elder years; I believe at the time of this resource being published she's in her eighties). It's interesting to note that Judith based her book on a real boy who actually grew up to be a community project lender for a bank!

Ideas for Parents

You can use this lesson at home with your child just as it is written here. Read the book in this lesson at home with your child. Encourage discussions about the consequences of not saving money. Have your child share his or her letter with your family.

For further insights on helping your child understand that once money is spent, it's gone, see the section, Additional Ideas for Parents, page 125. See also the Letter to the Parents, page 234.

Alexander's Money

Recording Sheet

Name _____

Place all your coins on the graph. Count the coins and record:

Alexander had _____ dimes, worth _____ cents.

Alexander had _____ nickels, worth _____ cents.

Alexander had _____ pennies, worth _____ cents.

How much were Alexander's coins worth altogether? _____

Dimes						
Nickels						
Pennies						

Listen to Alexander's story. As he spends his money, remove it from your graph.

A Letter to Alexander

Name _____

Dear Alexander,

_____

_____

_____

_____

_____

_____

_____

_____

May I Have Tomatoes for Cilantro?

A lesson on bartering for young learners

Overview

How can Maria Lili and her grandmother Mama Ana make chicken sancocho when all they have is eggs? Mama Ana knows a way. Considered "a case study in bartering genius," the children's book *Saturday Sancocho* takes children on a delightful journey through a food market as Mama Ana barters and trades for ingredients to make the popular South American stew chicken sancocho. A twist on getting everything, the story launches students into a graphing activity; upon a second reading of the book, students use cubes to represent the various ingredients. As ingredients are traded, students adjust the cube representations on their class graph. Mathematically the lesson provides practice in counting, adding and subtracting, and representing and interpreting data; it's appropriate for every age and ability. Students gain a deeper understanding of the difference in purchasing something versus bartering for it—and also get a special insight into the ingredient cumin.

Mathematics Goals

Students will:
► count to know how many
► add and subtract to know how many
► represent and interpret data

Economics Goals

Students will show:
► understanding of the Concept of Goods and Services by:
  • explaining the difference in purchasing and bartering for goods and services

Time

1 class period

Common Core State Standards for Mathematics:

Counting and Cardinality   K.CC.4.a.b.c.5
• *Count to tell the number of objects*

Operations and Algebraic Thinking   1.OA.5.6
• *Add and subtract within 20*

Measurement and Data   1.MD.4
• *Represent and interpret data*

Measurement and Data   2.MD.10
• *Represent and interpret data*

Literature Connections

Saturday Sancocho by Leyla Torres

Materials

snap cubes: 12 white, 13 green, 4 purple, 6 yellow, 8 orange, 4 brown, 12 red, 4 light green, 5 black

Graph Labels (Reproducible 4.4)

a real sample of the seasoning cumin

Teaching Directions

Part 1: Reading the Book

1. Gather students in the whole-group area of your classroom. Read the book *Saturday Sancocho* to students, making sure they can see the illustrations.

Part 2: Graphing Trades

2. Explain to students that you will be reading the story again. This time, they will be graphing the trading of food in the story. To prepare the graph, line up the graph labels (Reproducible 4.4) on the chalk ledge of your board. Show students the cubes; explain that each cube color will represent an ingredient in the story. Students will place cubes above the corresponding label, creating a graph that changes as trades are made in the book.

3. Hand out cubes to students—at least one cube per student if possible (see Materials list). As you hand out the cubes, review the directions with students. For example, hand out twelve red cubes and say, "these represent tomatoes" or four purple cubes and say, "these represent cassava."

4. Begin reading *Saturday Sancocho* again. Stop when Maria Lili places eggs in the basket. Ask students, "How many eggs are in a dozen?" Identify those students who are holding white cubes. Have them snap their cubes together and place the cube stick over the Egg label.

5. Continue reading. Stop when there is the trade of six eggs for plantains. Identify those thirteen students who are holding green cubes. Have them snap their cubes together and place the cube stick over the Plantain label.

6. Ask students, "What did Mama Ana trade to get the plantains?" When students respond that Mama Ana traded six eggs, have students help you count six white cubes and remove them from the graph. Ask students what they notice about the graph. Expect such responses as "there are more plantains than eggs" and "there are only cubes representing eggs and plantains."

Teaching Insight:
Picture Books
When reading picture books in whole-group settings, consider using a document camera or some form of technology that will project the illustrations for the whole class to more easily see.

Teaching Insight:
Snap Cubes Substitute
If you do not have a supply of cubes, cut corresponding colors of paper into 2-inch squares (use tape to affix the squares to the graph) or use assorted colors of sticky notes.

Teaching Insight:
Vocabulary in *Saturday Sancocho*
There are several words in this book that may need to be defined. *Sancocho* is a traditional soup or stew that is made in Latin American and Spanish countries. *Cassava* is a yucca plant. In the tropical and subtropical regions of the world it is grown as an annual crop. Its edible tuberous root is a major source of carbohydrates. Cassava is often used in soups. *Plantains* look like bananas but usually need to be cooked to be edible. They are not as sweet as bananas; in tropical regions of the world plantains are treated much like potatoes, cooked by boiling or frying them. A typical sancocho has plantains and cassava in addition to other ingredients.

7. Continue reading. On the next page Mama Ana trades nine plantains for four pounds of cassava. Identify those students who are holding purple cubes. Have them snap their cubes together and place the cube stick over the Cassava label.

8. Ask students, "What was traded to get the cassava?" When students respond that nine plantains were traded, have students help you count and remove nine plantains from the graph. Ask students what they now notice about the graph.

9. Continue reading. On the next page Mama Ana trades two pounds of cassava for six ears of corn. She also gives two eggs. Identify those six students who are holding yellow cubes. Have them snap their cubes together and place the cube stick over the Corn label.

10. Ask students, "What was traded to get the corn?" Have students help you remove two purple cubes (representing cassava) and two white cubes (representing eggs) from the graph. Ask students to tell you something true about the graph. At this point you should have four eggs, four plantains, two cassava, and six corn. Students may observe that eggs and plantains are the same. They may also observe that cassava has the least and corn has the most.

11. Continue reading. On the next page Mama Ana trades three ears of corn for eight carrots. Students holding orange cubes should snap their cubes together and place the cube stick above the Carrot label. Three yellow cubes (corn) should then be removed. Ask students what they notice about the graph now.

12. In the next trade Mama Ana trades the remaining eggs for onions and tomatoes. Have students with red cubes snap their cubes together and place the cube stick above the Tomato label. Do the same with students who have brown cubes (onions). Remove the remaining white cubes over the Egg label.

13. On the same page, Mama Ana trades tomatoes for cilantro. The author doesn't specify the number of tomatoes. Considering the recipe and the division of vegetables later in the story, at this time remove four tomato (red) cubes when you add the four cilantro (light green) cubes.

14. Continue reading. When the trade happens with cilantro (light green cubes) for garlic (black cubes), remove two cilantro and add five garlic cubes to the graph.

15. You are now nearing the end of the story. On the same page, garlic is traded for cumin. Because the recipe calls for two cloves of garlic, remove only one black cube for the trade for cumin. This time, have a container of ground cumin to share with students. Open the container and put a little cumin on a dish. Cumin is one of the most popular spices in the world. It has a distinct smell. Have students pass it around. It is used as a seasoning to add flavor to many Mexican recipes for soups and stews. There is no place on the graph for cumin—but isn't it interesting to smell?

Part 3: Revisiting the Concept of Bartering

16. To conclude the lesson, revisit the graph. Notice what is left. Ask students to tell you how the graph changed as trades were made. Point out that we started with only white cubes representing eggs and ended up with the ingredients needed for soup. Finish reading the book.

17. Ask students, "What did Mama Ana do when she had no money for the supplies for her sancocho?" Ask students if they remember what it is called when you trade instead of use money to get the things you need. Write the word *barter* where everyone can see it and facilitate a discussion about bartering (refer back to Lesson 1.1 in which students are first introduced to the concept of bartering via a look at the history of money).

Ideas for Parents

You can use this lesson at home with your child just as it is written here. Read the book in this lesson at home with your child. The recipe for sancocho is included in the back of the book; follow up with a trip to your local grocery store to buy the ingredients and make the soup with your child. When you are at your grocery store, make sure you include your child in the process of price comparison and making decisions about what to buy.

For further insights on helping your child understand that once money is spent, it's gone, see the section, Additional Ideas for Parents, page 125. See also the Letter to the Parents, page 234.

Graph Labels

Photocopy and enlarge these labels for everyone to see. Consider copying each label on a color of paper that matches the ingredient's cube color per the following list.

Eggs	white	Onions	brown
Plantains	green	Tomatoes	red
Cassava	purple	Cilantro	light green
Corn	yellow	Garlic	black
Carrots	orange	Cumin (no cubes)	

Eggs

Plantains

Cassava

Corn

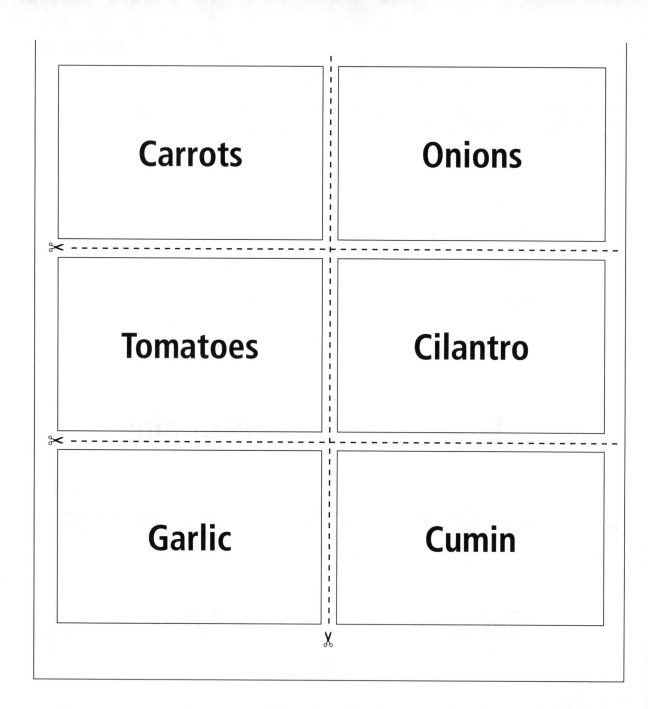

Carrots

Onions

Tomatoes

Cilantro

Garlic

Cumin

What Will We Find in the Store Today?

A counting and graphing lesson for young learners

Overview

As in Lesson 4.4, this lesson uses cubes to represent various foods. It continues to enrich students' data collection skills, providing an opportunity to build a graph that reflects the answer to the question, "What's in the store today?" Students pull cubes from a sock. A red cube represents the need for a sticky note to be added to the Tomato column of the graph, a yellow cube represents the need for a sticky note to be added to the Corn column of the graph, and so forth. Students practice representing and interpreting data, adding and subtracting, and ultimately build their awareness of the ever-changing nature of food supply on grocery store shelves (why can't grocery stores have everything?!). Use this lesson after students have read and are familiar with the book *Saturday Sancocho* (see Lesson 4.4).

Common Core State Standards for Mathematics:

Counting and Cardinality   K.CC.4.a.b.c.5
- *Count to tell the number of objects*

Operations and Algebraic Thinking   1.OA.5.6
- *Add and subtract within 20*

Measurement and Data   1.MD.4
- *Represent and interpret data*

Measurement and Data   2.MD.10
- *Represent and interpret data*

Mathematics Goals

Students will:
- ▶ count to know how many
- ▶ add and subtract to know how many
- ▶ represent and interpret data

Economics Goals

Students will show:
- ▶ understanding of the Concept of Goods and Services by:
  - •identifying that people are buyers and sellers of goods and services
- ▶ understanding of the Concept of Wants and Needs by:
  - •explaining that individuals and families cannot have everything they want

Time

1 class period

Materials

Classroom Graph (Reproducible 4.5), 1 enlarged copy for everyone in the class to see, plus individual copies for each pair of students for the extended lesson

sticky notes

socks containing 1 white snap cube, 1 green cube, 1 red cube, 1 orange cube, and 1 yellow cube, 1 set/sock for each pair or small group of students for the extended lesson

Literature Connections

Saturday Sancocho by Leyla Torres

Teaching Directions

Before you begin this lesson, make a classroom graph using Reproducible 4.5 as a model.

Part 1: Introducing and Modeling the Lesson

1. Gather students in the whole-group area of your classroom. Ask students, "Have you ever shopped in a store for food?" Most students have. Ask, "What do you buy when you go to a grocery store?" There should be a variety of answers. Explain to students that they are going to pretend they're taking a trip to the store. Ask students if they always find the same fruits and vegetables at the grocery store. Explain that sometimes fruits or vegetables are out of season so we can't always find everything. Fruits such as cherries grow and ripen in the summertime and aren't usually found in the grocery store in the winter. Sometimes we can't have everything we want to buy because the store is out or the item is out of season!

2. Remind students of the book *Saturday Sancocho*. Explain to students that they will be building another class graph representing food in a store. "What will we find in the store today?" Show students a sock containing a set of cubes (see Materials list). Explain that the cubes in the sock are different colors, representing the ingredients on the graph as follows (this is the same color scheme as used in Lesson 4.4):

Plantains	green	Carrots	orange
Tomatoes	red	Corn	yellow

3. Model how students need to reach into the sock and pull out one cube. What color is the cube? If it is a red cube, for example, place a sticky note in the Tomato column of the graph. If it is an orange cube, place a sticky note in the Carrot column of the graph. Continue modeling until students understand that the graph is built by putting one sticky note below the other in the appropriate column.

4. Make sure you draw a white cube during modeling. When a white cube is drawn, tell students that the white cube signals time to count how many sticky notes are beneath each label on the graph. Have the students together ask, "What will we find in the store today?" Students should then read the quantities on

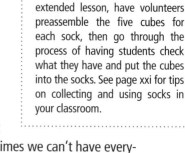

Teaching Insight:
Preparing the Socks
For the first part of this lesson, the whole-group setting, you'll need just one sock. For the extended lesson, have volunteers preassemble the five cubes for each sock, then go through the process of having students check what they have and put the cubes into the socks. See page xxi for tips on collecting and using socks in your classroom.

Teaching Insight:
Sampling with Replacement
As students play this game, the quantities will change between white cube draws, when students must read the quantities. Mathematicians would call this sampling with replacement. As long as quantities are five or less, have students just say the amount. This gives students an opportunity to instantly recognize a quantity. When there are more than five sticky notes in a column, have students quickly count as well. An example would be: "three plantains; two tomatoes; one, two, three, four, five, six carrots; and one corn."

the graph. For example, students might say, "three plantains, two tomatoes, no carrots, and one corn."

Part 2: Building the Graph

5. Have students play the game in a whole-group setting. Give each student an opportunity to draw a cube from the sock and place a sticky note in the corresponding column of the graph. Each time a cube is drawn, make sure it is returned to the sock. When every child has had an opportunity to pull a cube from the sock, the game is over. Do a final count on the graph. Consider asking the key questions here.

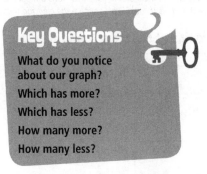

Key Questions

What do you notice about our graph?

Which has more?

Which has less?

How many more?

How many less?

Extensions

Extend this lesson by asking pairs of students to draw cubes from a sock and post their results on individual copies of the graph (Reproducible 4.5). Give each pair of students a sock with the five cubes as indicated in the Materials list, plus a copy of the graph. Tell students that when a color is drawn, they should place an "X" in the corresponding box (label) on their graph. When students draw the white cube, the process remains the same as in the whole-group activity. Students say, "What will we find in the store today?" and then count the number of Xs in the boxes.

After the boxes in one category are complete, students stop and write what they notice on their graph. For example, if there are two plantains, five tomatoes, one carrot, and two corn, students may write equations that indicate that there are fewer carrots than tomatoes (1 carrot < 5 tomatoes), or that there are the same amount of plantains as corn (2 plantains = 2 corn). Model on the board and encourage students to use the symbols <, >, and =.

Young children will enjoy doing this data collection more than once. Collect data on several days when you have a few extra minutes. If you use menus or math stations, this activity can be used with a small group of students.

Ideas for Parents

Consider using labels and colored magnets on your refrigerator to complete the graph at home with your child. Continue with the sampling until more than one column must be counted rather than instantly recognized.

For further insights on helping your child understand that once money is spent, it's gone, see the section, Additional Ideas for Parents, page 125. See also the Letter to the Parents, page 234.

Classroom Graph

Copy and enlarge this graph for classroom use or use it as a model to make your own graph. Columns in the graph should be 3 inches wide. Add pictures above the labels if you'd like. Laminate the classroom graph for future reuse. Make copies for individual use.

What will we find at the store today?

Plantains	Tomatoes	Carrots	Corn

From Why Can't I Have Everything? Teaching Today's Children to Be Financially and Mathematically Savvy, Grades PreK–2 by Jane Crawford.
© 2011 by Scholastic Inc. Permission granted to photocopy for nonprofit use in a classroom or similar place dedicated to face-to-face educational instruction.

The Grab and Go! Game

A lesson in comparing values of coins for young learners

Overview

This game is a new take on the *Matching* game (Lesson 1.3). Students play in partners, randomly pulling coins from a sock as quickly as possible. Partners then compare their coins and decide who has more money. They use the *Grab and Go!* recording sheet to record the coins each of them have and the total value. They then compare their coins, using the symbols <, >, or = to show the comparison. Play this game after students have had repeated experiences with Lesson 1.3.

Common Core State Standards for Mathematics:

Counting and Cardinality   K.CC.6
- *Compare numbers*

Number and Operations in Base Ten   1.NBT.2.a.b.c.3
- *Understand place value*

Number and Operations in Base Ten   2.NBT.4
- *Understand place value*

Measurement and Data   2.MD.8
- *Work with time and money*

Mathematics Goals

Students will:
- ▶ compare two numbers
- ▶ use place value understanding to add coin values
- ▶ solve problems involving money

Time

1 class period

Materials

socks filled with 3 pennies, 3 nickels, 3 dimes, and 2 quarters, 1 sock for each student

Grab and Go! Recording Sheet (Reproducible 4.6a), 1 copy per student

Grab and Go! Game Directions (Reproducible 4.6b), 1 copy per student

Teaching Insight:
Sets of Coins

For younger students, consider using only pennies, nickels, and dimes—or only pennies and dimes.

Teaching Insight:
Using Socks

You may wish to have students put coins into the socks. If coins are already in each sock, always start the lesson by having students take coins out to make sure they have all eleven coins. See page xxi for more tips on collecting and using socks in your classroom.

Teaching Directions

Part 1: Introducing and Modeling the Game

1. Have a volunteer be your partner and model playing the game with you. Explain that this game is a new way of playing the *Matching* game (Lesson 1.3). Students will play in partners. Have your partner get ready. Say, "ready, set, go!" Both of you must quickly pull three coins from your socks (grabbing coins should be done quickly so students don't have the opportunity to select the coins). Compare your coins with your partner and decide who has more money. Ask the key questions.

2. Show students the *Grab and Go!* Recording Sheet (Reproducible 4.6a). Record the coins each of you have and their total value. Use <, >, or = to show the comparison. Return all coins to the socks.

Part 2: Playing the Game

3. Give each student a coin-filled sock (see Materials list) and a copy of the *Grab and Go!* Recording Sheet (Reproducible 4.6a) (for those students at the appropriate reading level, consider also giving them the game's directions plus a couple of bonus steps; see Reproducible 4.6b). Have students count to make sure there are eleven coins in each of their socks. Students play the game in partners. Circulate while the students are playing, observing and taking note of any challenges students may have.

Key Questions

Whose coins are worth the most?

Whose coins are worth the least?

Teaching Insight: Recording
When students are playing the game for the first time, or if students with very little money-counting experience are playing, you might want to tell students to play without recording. Afterward students can record and will be able to practice using the signs <, >, and =.

Extensions

Extend the lesson for second graders by asking how much money they have with all eleven coins. They can also be asked to determine how much more they need to make one dollar.

Consider sending students home with a copy of the game's directions (Reproducible 4.6b) so that they can play with their parents and family members.

Idea$ for Parent$

To adapt this game to play with your child at home, be your child's partner. Refer to the game's directions (Reproducible 4.6b). Play this game without use of the recording sheet first, then play using the recording sheet (Reproducible 4.6a). Follow the suggestions in the lesson regarding adjusting coins if your child is still struggling with coin recognition and coin values.

It is important to continue to assess your child's ability to recognize coins and understand values. Use the coins in your pocket or purse at the end of the day to determine whether your child can tell you the name of coins and what each coin value is.

For further insights on helping your child understand that once money is spent, it's gone, see the section, Additional Ideas for Parents, page 125. See also the Letter to the Parents, page 234.

Grab and Go!

Recording Sheet

Name _____

Name _____

Compare your coins with your partner and decode who has more. Record the coins each of you have and their total value. Use <, >, or = to show the comparison.

○ ○ ○ = _____ cents	<, >, =	○ ○ ○ = _____ cents
○ ○ ○ = _____ cents		○ ○ ○ = _____ cents
○ ○ ○ = _____ cents		○ ○ ○ = _____ cents
○ ○ ○ = _____ cents		○ ○ ○ = _____ cents

Grab and Go!

Game Directions

You need:

- 1 sock per player, each filled with two quarters, three dimes, three nickels, and three pennies

Directions:

1. Work with a partner. At the same time, say, "ready, set, go" and each quickly pull out three coins from your socks.

2. Hold your hand out and work with your partner to count your coins and your partner's coins.

3. Compare amounts. Whose coins are worth the most? Whose coins are worth the least? Show your coins and comparisons on the recording sheet.

Notes:

- Make sure you both agree on the value of your coins.

- Put the coins back into your socks after each turn.

- When you finish playing, make sure each sock has two quarters, three dimes, three nickels, and three pennies inside.

Bonus:

- Each time, figure out how much you and your partner have altogether.

- Can you figure out how much more you and your partner would need to have a dollar?

Formative Assessment

In this chapter students had an opportunity to think about why we can't have everything and the consequences when we spend without thinking. They made lists of wants and needs. Bartering is revisited within children's literature.

While students are working on the problems posed in this chapter's lessons, you may want to make the following observations:

- Were students able to name a few things that were *needs*?
- Were students able to name a few things that were *wants*?
- Were students able to connect to the idea that our needs are essential for life?
- Can students describe bartering?
- How did students count the coins when they played the *Grab and Go!* game?
- How did students decide which group of coins had a greater value?
- Were students able to make visual estimates about whose coins had a greater or lesser value?
- Did students use landmark numbers or friendlier numbers to determine how much money they had?
- Were students engaged in activities?

Students should be able to describe bartering. Students can draw a picture depicting bartering. Older students can include writing with their picture.

Students should be able to name a few things that are wants and a few things that are needs. Young children can draw pictures and older students can write or make wants and needs lists.

Students have opportunities to count coins. You should continue charting which students are able to count which coins.

Additional Idea$ for Parent$

Helping Your Child Be Financially Savvy with Spending Decisions

One important lesson about spending that we want our children to learn is that once money is spent, it is really gone. It is so easy to rescue our children when they spend all of their allowance and have no money for something they really want. When we give them money after they spend foolishly, we are teaching children to hurry and spend, without thinking and planning, because someone will help them out if something important comes along. I am not saying you shouldn't find a way for your child to earn extra money or borrow from future allowances. Payment for extra chores is a great way to fill the gap. Borrowing from future allowances may get too complicated.

Don't try to control your child's spending. Instead, consider asking the questions that appear here.

Sometimes we can just delay gratification so our children learn to think before spending. Questioning will help set this pattern. If your child chooses to spend foolishly on something that will break soon, don't say anything. Let your child learn about buying something foolishly. That doesn't mean that he or she can buy anything and spend everything—the basic household rules should still stand. If you have a rule such as no sugar, no paper dolls, or no toy guns, then even if your child has money, that rule stands. Perhaps make a rule that your child is to save a portion of her or his allowance as well (for more insights on giving your child an allowance, see Chapter 2, Additional Ideas for Parents, page 61).

Another way to reinforce smart spending with your child is to have him or her watch you compare prices when you shop. Talk through the process while you compare prices so that your child can be part of your decision making.

Remember, money management skills are learned mostly at home! See also the Letter to the Parents, page 234.

> ## Questions to Ask Your Child About His or Her Spending Decisions
>
> Is the thing you are about to buy something you really need or something you want?
>
> What is the quality? (For example, Will the thing you are about to buy be something that might break soon after you get it home?)
>
> Do you have something you really want that costs a little more that you could afford after your next allowance?
>
> How badly do you really want what you are about to buy?
>
> Is there something you would rather have?

CHAPTER 5

How Do We Earn Money?

Explore the Differences Between Goods and Services—Focusing on Earning Money and How It All Adds Up

Overview

Chapter 5 takes children's understanding of money to an even richer level, addressing the concept of *earning* money and helping to move students' understanding of sources of money beyond tooth fairies and allowances.

The literature in this chapter is some of the best yet, providing compelling, real-life contexts for thinking about situations where people earn money. In turn, students think about ways that they can earn money.

The chapter opens with **Lesson 5.1**, in which students are introduced to key financial terms such as *capital* and *revenue*. In **Lessons 5.2** and **5.3** they apply their business smarts to their personal experiences, collecting data on what their peers have done to earn money. These data open the door to a discussion on the differences between goods and services—concepts pivotal to students' understanding of "How do we earn money?" **Lessons 5.4** and **5.5** apply the concept of goods and services to multicultural, real-life situations. Students are gently reminded that earning money isn't just a means to provide for ourselves; it also can involve earning to share with others—perhaps best driven home through the true account of a child-led campaign to earn money in **Lesson 5.6**. Of course, to understand how we earn money, children must have a solid understanding of how it all adds up. Each lesson involves a mathematical focus—whether it be collecting and representing data, counting money, or working with place value. **Lesson 5.7** requires a culmination of students' mathematical skills, introducing them to the properties of addition through a gamelike approach.

The Lessons

Formative Assessment 160

Formative Assessment Activity 161

Formative Assessment Checklist 162

Literature Used in This Chapter

Arthur's Funny Money by Lillian Hoban

Jenny Found a Penny by Trudy Harris

Ox-Cart Man by Donald Hall

My Rows and Piles of Coins by Tololwa M. Mollel

Pennies for Elephants by Lita Judge

Additional Idea$ for Parent$

Arthur's Funny Money

Introducing basic business plan concepts to young learners

Overview

With a little brainstorming and a few soapy supplies from the store, Arthur starts his own bike-washing business, only to discover that the math gets complicated—does he charge the same for skateboards? Tricycles? And what about when the cost of supplies increases? Little sister Victoria comes to the rescue—provided Arthur helps her with her math problems. Let the story tell whether it's a fair trade! Simple business concepts are ingeniously woven throughout the delightful adventure *Arthur's Funny Money*. The book is part of the popular I Can Read Book series, standing the test of time, and appropriate for grades 1 through 3 reading levels. Once students read and discuss the book, examples of Arthur's business endeavors provide the context for introducing and exploring key business concepts—from *capital* and *revenue* to *earnings*—in child-friendly ways, in addition to providing a context for practicing mathematical skills in adding, subtracting, and solving money-related word problems. Students then start thinking about what business they would like to start—taking the initial step in building a business plan.

Mathematics Goals

Students will:
▶ use place value to add and subtract
▶ solve word problems involving money

Common Core State Standards for Mathematics:

Number and Operations in Base Ten   1.NBT.2.a.b.c
• *Understand place value*

Number and Operations in Base Ten   2.NBT.1.a.b.2.7
• *Understand place value*
• *Use place value understanding and properties of operations to add and subtract*

Measurement and Data 2.MD.8
• *Work with time and money*

Economics Goals

Students will show:
▶ understanding of the Concept of Earning Money by:
  • discussing that work provides income to purchase goods and services
▶ understanding of the Concept of Goods and Services by:
  • identifying examples of goods and services
  • identifying services that people provide
  • identifying that people are buyers and sellers of goods and services
  • discussing that people save money for future goods and services
▶ understanding of the Concept of Wants and Needs by:
  • explaining why wanting more than we have requires people to make choices

Literature Connections

Arthur's Funny Money by Lillian Hoban

Materials

paper and pencil for all students

Time

1 class period

Teaching Directions

Part 1: Introducing and Reading the Book

1. Gather students in the whole-group area of your classroom. Show your students the front cover of the book *Arthur's Funny Money*. Ask them to put their hand up if they think they know what Arthur and his sister are doing. Listen while a few students offer suggestions. Most will say Arthur is buying candy. Then ask, where do you think Arthur got his money? Listen to a few suggestions.

2. Read *Arthur's Funny Money* to students, making sure they can see the illustrations.

Part 2: Discussing the Book

3. When you are finished reading, discuss the story with students. Consider asking the key questions here, referring to the book to confirm the answers.

Part 3: Introducing, Exploring, and Discussing Business Concepts

4. Introduce the word *accountant* to students. Explain that an accountant is a person who helps figure out how much money people have. Tell students that they are going to pretend they are Arthur's accountants. They'll help Arthur figure out how much he ended up having to spend when buying soap and supplies at the store for his bike-washing business.

5. Start by writing *$3.78* where everyone can see it. Then introduce the first important business concept—the idea of *capital*. State, "Arthur had three dollars and seventy-eight cents in his piggy bank. People in business would describe that three dollars and seventy-eight cents as his *capital*. He spent fifty-three cents on a box of soap and twenty-seven cents on a box of Brillo. If we are his accountants, we have to figure out how much he spent on supplies."

6. Ask students to work with a partner to find the answer to the problem. Provide students with paper to record their thinking. You may notice that some students choose to draw pictures of coins. Other students might use the "making ten" strategy by adding three and seven.

> **Teaching Insight:**
> **Picture Books**
> When reading picture books in whole-group settings, consider using a document camera or some form of technology that will project the illustrations for the whole class to more easily see.

Key Questions

What did Arthur want?

How much did it cost?

Who had ideas for earning money?

What were those ideas?

What did Arthur finally decide to do?

Is washing bikes a good or a service?

What makes washing bikes a service?

Did Arthur have to buy anything to do this service? What did he buy?

How much money did Arthur have to spend on supplies?

What did Arthur have to do so people would know he was washing bikes?

Was that his only advertising?

Did Arthur earn enough money to buy his T-shirt and cap?

7. Reconvene students as a whole group and discuss their different approaches to the problem. Consider asking the key questions here.

8. Next, ask students to think about the business concept of *revenue*. State, "Norman paid Arthur forty-two cents for washing the bike and trike. Wilma gave Arthur thirty-four cents. Peter gave Arthur thirty-six cents. John gave Arthur thirty-three cents. How much money (*revenue*) did Arthur make?" Give students paper and ask them to choose to work alone or with a partner to figure out how much Arthur earned.

9. When students find an answer, discuss how they solved the problem. Use the same key questions as in Step 7 and record students' strategies in a list for everyone to see.

10. Have students look at Arthur's expenses and his earnings. Consider asking the key questions here.

11. Reread pages 54 and 55 of the book, where Arthur figures out how much money he has. Ask students, "Was Arthur a good accountant? Did he have enough money to buy the T-shirt and cap for four dollars and twenty-five cents?"

12. Tell students the T-shirt cost five dollars originally. Ask them, "How much was the price reduced? How did you figure that out?"

Part 4: Thinking About a Business Plan

13. When Arthur started thinking about making money, he had to think of several things. Ask students, "If we were going to start a business to make some money, what would we have to consider?" Listen to students give their ideas. Talk with students about creating a business plan. Such a plan might start with an idea to earn money. It would include a list of needs in order to accomplish the task and an estimate of how much the goods would cost. There should be some capital investment to cover those start-up costs. Students should think of a way to let people know about their business. They need to tell how much their good or service costs. Finally, they need to plan for a way to keep their money safe.

Key Questions

How did you solve the problem?

Did you think about the problem in another way? Explain.

Teaching Insight: Varying the Task

Younger children definitely need to partner on this large of a problem. For younger children, you might adapt the task to be "Did Arthur earn more or less than a dollar?"

Key Questions

Did Arthur make money or lose money? How much money?

Why didn't Arthur buy more soap and Brillo?

The Brillo was fifty-three cents in the morning and sixty-four cents in the afternoon. How much did the price go up?

Part 5: Introducing the Final Project

14. This point in the lesson is a good time to bring up the final project to students. Tell students that they are going to have an opportunity to earn money later (see the Final Project, page 239). They should start thinking about ideas for making a good or doing a service. Send the parent letter on page 238 home with students, alerting parents of a future money-earning project.

Financial Facts

Capital **has several meanings.** Capital is the money a company has to finance its operation and use to make more money.

Revenue **is the money that a business gets from the sale of goods and services to its customers.**

Earnings **are what are left when expenses are subtracted from revenues.**

Capital, revenue, **and** *earnings* **are not common vocabulary for young children.** However, if students are able to use complicated dinosaur names, they can certainly be exposed to the proper economics terms—as long as there is a reasonable context for using this vocabulary! (Note that young students should not, however, be tested on these terms.)

Idea$ for Parent$

You can use this lesson at home with your child just as it is written here; you will need to be your child's discussion and activity partner. Read the book in this lesson at home with your child. Encourage discussions about basic business concepts. The lesson is appropriate for all ability levels. If your child is very young, follow the suggestions for younger children. If adding amounts is difficult for your child, take the role of accountant and talk through the steps as you add the numbers.

For further insights on helping your child learn the true value of a dollar via opportunities to earn money, see the section, Additional Ideas for Parents, page 162. See also the Letter to the Parents, page 235.

Have You Ever Been Paid for Doing Something?

A data collection lesson connecting personal experiences to the concept of earning money for young learners

Overview

In Lesson 5.1 students learned of Arthur's experience in earning money; Lesson 5.2 takes the concepts in the previous lesson to a more personal depth, giving students the opportunity to share ways that they themselves have earned money. Students work as a whole group to establish a method for collecting data in answer to the question "Have you ever been paid for doing something?" Then they work in partners to explore ways that they can represent the data they've collected. To conclude, they reconvene as a group and share their various strategies, providing a forum for mathematically and financially rich discussions. This lesson works best with most first and second graders.

Mathematics Goals

Students will:
▶ represent and interpret data

Common Core State Standards for Mathematics:

Measurement and Data   1.MD.4
  • *Represent and interpret data*
Measurement and Data   2.MD.10
  • *Represent and interpret data*

Economics Goals

Students will show:
▶ understanding of the Concept of Earning Money by:
  • discussing different types of jobs that people do

Materials

list of all students' names, 1 copy per student
paper and pencil for all students

Time

1 class period

Literature Connections

Arthur's Funny Money by Lillian Hoban

Teaching Directions

Part 1: Connecting to Literature

1. Gather students in the whole-group area of your classroom. Hold up a copy of *Arthur's Funny Money* (students should already be familiar with this book from its use in Lesson 5.1). Tell your students to think about jobs they have done to earn money. Ask, "Has anyone ever washed bikes to earn money—the same job as Arthur?" There may not be anyone who has washed bikes. Ask, "Has anyone ever been paid for doing something? If so, what?" Listen while students tell their stories about earning money in a job and/or doing a task for someone.

Part 2: Introducing and Collecting the Data

2. Explain to students that you are interested in knowing how many of them worked and were paid; you'd like to keep track of what they're saying. Suggest they record the data.

3. Start by distributing copies of your class roster (list of students' names). Ask students to look at the list. Display a master copy of the list so that everyone can see it.

4. Tell students you are going to ask everyone on the list the same question. When they hear the answer, everyone needs to record it so they will be able to tell who said "yes" and who said "no." Ask students how they think they can best record the information. Take suggestions, such as making Yes and No columns on their lists and placing a mark to show "yes" or "no" after each student's name.

5. Call out students' names from the list one at a time and ask, "Have you ever been paid for doing something for someone?" The corresponding student needs to answer "yes" or "no." Go slowly so students are able to record the responses.

Part 3: Representing the Data

6. When everyone has responded, ask students to work with their partners. Explain that their task is to represent this data in some way. They can use pictures, words, and/or numbers. They can use cubes, paper, or other materials in the classroom. Explain that it is important to make a way for people to know the question that was asked; they need to show the information *and* the responses. If they just make snap-cube trains, for example, without making some kind of card, there is no way to know if each student answered "yes" or "no."

7. Circulate as students are working, observing and making notes of any challenges. As students finish, look at their work and ask them to add a clarifying sentence if their information needs further explanation.

Part 4: Processing the Data

8. When everyone has finished, display everyone's work for the class to see. Reconvene as a whole group and discuss students' various strategies. Listen to students; then consider asking the key questions.

Key Questions

What way did you show how many students have and have not been paid for doing tasks? Explain.

Does anyone have a different way of showing this information? Explain.

Idea$ for Parent$

This lesson requires collecting data and then finding a way to represent it. In lieu of classroom data collection, help your child survey a small circle of friends or young relatives. Choose a way to display the data. You may want to build a bar graph showing responses to every category.

For further insights on helping your child learn the true value of a dollar via opportunities to earn money, see the section, Additional Ideas for Parents, page 162. See also the Letter to the Parents, page 235.

Goods and Services

A data collection lesson in understanding the concept of goods and services for young learners

Overview

Building on the previous two lessons in this chapter, this lesson connects the concept of earning money to children's personal experiences, this time asking them to think about what it is exactly they've done to earn money (for students who haven't earned money, don't worry!—there is also an opportunity for them to participate). Students revisit the book *Jenny Found a Penny* (this book is originally introduced in the lessons in Chapter 3) as the context for thinking about jobs they've done. They then use their mathematical skills to collect and represent their data. The data opens the door to a discussion on the differences between goods and services—further expanding students' financial savvy and awareness of the answer to the question "How do we earn money?"

Economics Goals

Students will show:
- ▶ understanding of the Concept of Earning Money by:
  - • discussing different types of jobs that people do
- ▶ understanding of the Concept of Goods and Services by:
  - • identifying examples of goods and services
  - • identifying services that people provide

Common Core State Standards for Mathematics:

Measurement and Data   1.MD.4
- • *Represent and interpret data*

Measurement and Data   2.MD.10
- • *Represent and interpret data*

Mathematics Goal

Students will:
- ▶ represent and interpret data

Materials

sticky notes

Time

30 minutes

Literature Connections

Jenny Found a Penny by Trudy Harris

Teaching Directions

Part 1: Connecting to Literature

1. Gather students in the whole-group area of your classroom. Revisit the book *Jenny Found a Penny*. Ask students, "Can anyone remember how Jenny got her money?" Listen while students tell about the jobs Jenny had and the ways she found money. As students recall Jenny's jobs, create a list where all students can see it, writing each job at the top of the list, horizontally, and leaving substantial space underneath (this is in anticipation of the graph that will be built in Part 3).

Part 2: Connecting to Students' Lives

2. Tell students that you want to know if anyone has done any of the same jobs that Jenny did. Listen while students share. Some students may have done more than one of Jenny's jobs. Emphasize that they are going to be able to contribute only one response to the forthcoming task, even though they might have done more than one of the things listed; they should choose the job they have done the most!

Part 3: Collecting and Representing Data

3. Give each student a sticky note. Ask students to put something on the sticky note that represents their chosen response to the question "What job on Jenny's list have you done?" The representations can be in words or pictures.

4. Send a few students at a time to post their sticky notes under the corresponding job on the list you've created in Step 1, ultimately building a graph. When all of the sticky notes have been posted, ask students if they can help you title the graph. If they don't suggest it, add the title "What job have you done?" to the top of the graph.

Teaching Insight:
Gathering Genuine Responses

The purpose of having children put something indicating their response on sticky notes is to help students actually follow their response to the question, rather than responding to the category that seems to be in the majority with their peers. Young children sometimes are swayed by the data posted by others. Consequently, when it is their turn to post their job they will join the winning column instead of posting the job they have done the most. However, when they have a representation or word defining their job, they usually will post to the column showing their job.

Teaching Insight:
Selecting Jobs

Babysitting, sweeping, and vacuuming aren't the only jobs Jenny did to earn money. When considering the data collection question "What job on Jenny's list have you done?", keep in mind that you are trying to collect a good assortment of responses while simultaneously limiting the categories. Too many choices might lead to only one or two responses in each category. Limiting the categories to four or five, including a "none" category for students who have not done tasks to earn money, should give enough data for a discussion. If students insist, you can include feeding the dog, washing dishes, folding clothes, vacuuming, babysitting, and sweeping.

Part 4: Processing the Data

5. After everyone has posted her or his response, consider asking the key questions.

6. After students have finished talking about the graph, ask students, "Why do we want to work?" You might hear that they want to get money to buy something. Take this opportunity to explain that we fill our wants and needs by earning money to buy goods. Goods are things we can see and touch. Clothing and food are both considered goods. Electronic games and cell phones are also goods. Anything we buy that we can touch is considered a good.

7. After discussing the concept of goods, give students an explanation of what *services* are in comparison to goods. Sometimes we pay for things we can't touch. Those things are services. I pay someone to cut my hair. That is a service. Your dentist and doctor also perform a service. Services are work that is done for other people. We get paid for services we perform. Ask students, "Is babysitting a good or a service? What about sweeping? Why is that a service? Can anyone name another service besides the ones we put on the list?"

Key Questions

What do you notice about the data we've collected?

What can we learn from this data?

How many responses did we have in all? How do you know?

How does the number of responses compare to the students in our classroom?

What could a visitor to our classroom tell about us from looking at this graph?

How many more . . . ?

How many less . . . ?

Which had the most? (Connect the word *mode* to the one that has the most; see Lesson 2.7 for more insights on teaching the term *mode*.)

Financial Facts

Goods are things we can see and touch—they are things that are made. Clothing and food are both considered goods. Electronic games and cell phones are also goods. Anything we buy that we can touch is considered a good.

Services are things we pay for but can't touch. Hair stylists, dentists, and doctors all perform services. Services are work that is done for other people. We get paid for services we perform.

Idea$ for Parent$

With a few modifications you can successfully use this lesson outside of the classroom. Help your child record two or three headings (jobs) on a paper. Help your child call or visit friends to collect information about which job they have done. Be sure to review the jobs in the book *Jenny Found a Penny* to help your child build understanding about the difference in goods and services.

For further insights on helping your child learn the true value of a dollar via opportunities to earn money, see the section, Additional Ideas for Parents, page 162. See also the Letter to the Parents, page 235.

Ox-Cart Man

A lesson connecting survival needs to the concept of earning money for young learners

Overview

A Caldecott Medal winner, the book *Ox-Cart Man* takes readers on a comforting journey through the yearly passage of one man and his family selling goods to earn a living. From mittens, shawls, and birch brooms to potatoes, feathers, and ultimately his ox, the man sells goods that have been handmade, raised, and/or grown on his farm in historical New England. When he has coins in his pocket, he then buys things to take home to his family. This is a gorgeously illustrated tale that reaps financial lessons as well as an awareness of survival needs, self-sufficiency, family relationships, history, and the circle of life. This lesson connects the story to key economic ideas, further supporting students in answering the question "How do we earn money?" In whole-group and partner settings, students explore the concept of goods, income, and buyers and sellers, simultaneously practicing mathematical skills in estimation and counting. Though the mathematical goals focus on counting (kindergarten), this lesson is appropriate for children of all ability levels; its unsurpassable strengths reside in the economics goals.

Mathematics Goal

Students will:
▶ count to tell how many

Common Core State Standard for Mathematics:

Counting and Cardinality   K.CC.5
  • *Count to tell the number of objects*

Economics Goals

Students will show:
▶ understanding of the Concept of Money by:
  • identifying that people use money to purchase goods and services
▶ understanding of the Concept of Earning Money by:
  • discussing that people make goods and perform services
  • discussing that work provides income to purchase goods and services
▶ understanding of the Concept of Goods and Services by:
  • identifying examples of goods and services
  • identifying goods that people make
  • identifying that people are buyers and sellers of goods and services
  • discussing that people save money for future goods and services

Materials

chart paper or some means of displaying written lists for students to see

Time

1 class period

Literature Connections

Ox-Cart Man by Donald Hall

Teaching Directions

Part 1: Introducing and Reading the Book

1. Gather students in the whole-group area of your classroom. Before you begin reading *Ox-Cart Man*, talk to students about where and when this story takes place. Use a map or a globe to show students where New England is located. Refer to how near or far you live from the New England states. Tell students that the story took place long, long ago when America was young. The story begins in the month of October. When students look at the first illustrations in the book, they will notice the leaves are changing colors.

> **Teaching Insight:**
> **Picture Books**
> When reading picture books in whole-group settings, consider using a document camera or some form of technology that will project the illustrations for the whole class to more easily see.

2. Read *Ox-Cart Man* to students, making sure they can see the illustrations.

Part 2: Estimating and Counting Items

3. After you've read the book through once, ask students, "How many things did the man take with him to sell?" Have students estimate their answers. Give students time—a minute or two—to silently think to themselves. Then tell them to share their thinking with the person next to them.

4. Using a means for everyone in the classroom to see what you write (e.g., chart paper), record students' estimates. Then ask students to recall some of the items. List those items for everyone to see as well. Examples may include:

Items the Man Took to Sell

- a bag of wool
- a shawl his wife made
- five pairs of mittens
- candles
- shingles
- potatoes
- apples
- honey and honeycombs
- turnips
- cabbages
- maple sugar
- a bag of goose feathers
- the wooden box he carried the maple sugar in
- the barrel he carried the apples in
- the bag he carried the potatoes in
- his ox cart
- his ox
- his ox's yoke and harness

5. With your students, count the items on the list. Students may have to make some decisions in the counting process; for example, they may need to decide if they want to count the five pairs of mittens as one item or five items, and if the honey and honeycombs are one item or two items.

6. Reread the section of the book that describes what the man sold so students can be sure they found all of the goods that were sold.

7. Now ask students, "How many things did the man buy with the money he had after he sold his items?" Repeat Steps 4 through 6, now applying the estimates and item lists to this question. Answers to the items the man bought may include an iron kettle, an embroidery needle, a Barlow knife, and/or two pounds of wintergreen peppermint candies. Go back to the book and reread the section listing the goods he bought.

Part 3: Discussing Economic Ideas

8. There are several economic ideas in this one story. The man and his family produce and harvest goods that are sold at market. The man gets money by selling items at the market. The man buys goods at market that he and his family aren't able to make. It isn't always possible to make and harvest all the things we need. The market is a place for people to buy and sell goods. Start a discussion of these economic ideas by asking the key questions shown here.

Key Questions

Did the man have a job?

Who did the man work for?

If the man didn't work for someone, how did he get money for the things he needed?

Why didn't the man and his family make the things he bought?

When the man got home, what did he begin working on?

What else did the man do?

What did the man's family make?

How did the family get maple sugar?

Where did the family get yarn?

What do you think the man will sell the next October?

Do you think the man had coins left after he made his purchases?

Why would the man save some money?

Idea$ for Parent$

You can use this lesson at home with your child just as it is written here; you will need to be your child's discussion and activity partner. Read the book in this lesson at home with your child. Encourage discussions about earning money in the context of survival needs.

For further insights on helping your child learn the true value of a dollar via opportunities to earn money, see the section, Additional Ideas for Parents, page 162. See also the Letter to the Parents, page 235.

My Rows and Piles of Money

A lesson in earning, saving, and sharing—and the importance of place value for young learners

Overview

This multiday lesson opens with an extensive money-counting activity; though the activity uses a counting jar, it is different from the other counting jar lessons in this book (Lessons 2.4 through 2.6). It gives students an opportunity to actively take part in estimating, sorting, counting, and finally grouping large amounts of coins by place value—ultimately forming rows and piles that then transition to the reading of the children's book *My Rows and Piles of Money*. In this heartwarming story, Saruni is saving money in his secret money box—not for the many delightful items in the market that would catch a child's eye (toy trucks, kites, and roasted peanuts, to name a few), but for something more special—a bicycle that will help his mother deliver her own items to the market. Saruni saves—and practices carrying goods on his father's bicycle—until he feels he has enough money to buy his mother her own bicycle. However, when Saruni goes to buy the bicycle, the bicycle vendor scornfully laughs at how little money he has. Saruni, his hopes dashed, returns home to his father, who surprisingly announces that the money is just enough to buy his bicycle (and then returns his son's money to him). A touching, selfless perspective on financial endeavors, the book *My Rows and Piles of Money* reminds students that earning money isn't just a means to provide for ourselves; it also can involve earning to share with others. The story continues the exploration of connections between earning money and buying and selling goods—this time with a cultural spin through Tanzania. To continue to explore the idea of sharing money versus spending or saving it, see the lessons in Chapter 6.

Mathematics Goals

Students will:
- ▶ count coins to determine how much money there is
- ▶ use place value to count coins
- ▶ work with equal groups to gain a foundation for multiplication
- ▶ understand place value
- ▶ solve problems involving money

Economics Goals

Students will show:
- ▶ understanding of the Concept of Money by:
  - • recognizing various forms of U.S. currency
  - • recognizing that different countries have different coins
- ▶ understanding of the Concept of Goods and Services by:
  - • discussing that people save money for future goods and services

Common Core State Standards for Mathematics:

Counting and Cardinality   K.CC.1.4.a.b.c.5.7
- • *Know number names and the count sequence*
- • *Count to tell the number of objects*
- • *Compare numbers*

Number and Operations in Base Ten   1. NBT.1.2.a.b.c
- • *Extend the counting sequence*
- • *Understand place value*

Operations and Algebraic Thinking   2.OA.4
- • *Work with equal groups of objects to gain foundations for multiplication*

Number and Operations in Base Ten   2. NBT.1.a.b.2.3
- • *Understand place value*

Measurement and Data   2.MD.8
- • *Work with time and money*

Materials

a jar of coins containing more than 1 dollar each in pennies, nickels, dimes,
quarters, and half-dollars—but totaling less than 10 dollars

poster-sized paper (newsprint, butcher paper, or 17-by-11-inch copy paper),
3 sheets

solid-colored blanket

5 large paper plates or trays

5 labels (1 each: *half-dollar, quarter, dime, nickel,* and *penny*) to fit the paper
plates or trays

a small supply of dimes and pennies for making trades of nickels on the place-
value chart

a camera to record the final groupings of rows and piles of coins

80 to 100 counting cups (small 1- to 3-ounce cups are ideal)

Ten-Frame Sheet (Reproducible 3.3), 10 copies (ideally on construction paper for
more durability)

extra supply of coins (in addition to above jar)

2 strips of paper for label purposes

digital camera or other photo-taking device for capturing final place-value chart,
Step 26

Time

a series of six days; each part
will take approximately
20 minutes

Teaching Insight:
**Varying the Number and
Types of Coins**

Keep in mind, the younger the
children, the smaller the jar. If
you are doing this lesson with
kindergarten students, you may
want to limit coins to pennies
and dimes. If you are working
with first graders later in the year,
go ahead with a good amount
of coins so everyone can have
some part in counting them. For
second-grade students, a large jar
with several dollars of each type
of coin will work best (as listed
in Materials). If using half-dollars,
for students who are unfamiliar
with half-dollars, make sure
you've done Lesson 3.1, *What's a
Half-Dollar?*, first.

Teaching Insight:
Blanket

A blanket is suggested in this
lesson to contain the spillage
of coins from the counting jar.
Anything that can be laid flat on
the floor and sufficiently collect
coins will do (e.g., a bed sheet);
simply make sure it's durable and
of a solid color (no pattern/print)
so the coins can be easily seen
when you count them with your
class.

Teaching Directions

Part 1: Estimating Money (Days 1–3)

1. Let students know that in this lesson they will ultimately be reading the story *My Rows and Piles of Coins*, but first in this multiday lesson they will be doing a money-counting activity.

2. Show students a jar of money (see the Materials list; make sure there is less than ten dollars in your jar).

3. Ask students to estimate how much money is in the jar. You may get reasonable estimates, or you may have lots of guesses, such as "a million dollars!"

4. Tell students you are going to leave the jar in the front of the classroom for a few days. (Be sure to tape the lid so students can't get into the jar.) Explain to them that when they find some time to study the jar, you want them to think about the answers to several key questions.

5. Explain that you are going to display two posters next to the jar for students to record their responses to the key questions. The posters should be as follows (see Figures 5–1 and 5–2).

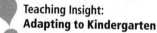

Teaching Insight:
Adapting to Kindergarten
As stated in the Teaching Insight next to the Materials list, if you are working with kindergarten students, limit the coins in the jar to dimes and pennies. Have students refrain from thinking about the value of the coins; they should focus on estimating the number of dimes and pennies in the jar.

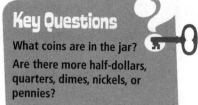

Key Questions

What coins are in the jar?

Are there more half-dollars, quarters, dimes, nickels, or pennies?

What do you think is the total value of all the coins?

What Coins Are in the Jar?

Do you think there are more half-dollars, quarters, dimes, nickels, or pennies in the jar? Place an "X" below the coin that you think there are more of in the jar.

Half-dollars	Quarters	Dimes	Nickels	Pennies
X	X	X	X	X
	X	X	X	X
		X		X
		X		X
				X
				X
				X
				X

Figure 5–1. Poster 1 Example

What Is the Total Value of the Coins in the Jar?

What do you think the total value is of all the coins in the jar? Write your estimate in one of the boxes.

$5.00	$100.00	$4.00	$7.86	One million
$8,59				

Figure 5–2. Poster 2 Example

Part 2: Interpreting the Data (Day 4)

6. After students have recorded their responses on the two posters, explain that the responses to the question "What Coins Are in the Jar?" created a graph. Interpret the data with your class. Then, consider asking the key questions shown here.

7. Next, look at the second poster that asks, " What Is the Total Value of the Coins in the Jar?" Have students help you find the highest estimate and the lowest estimate; circle them. Ask students, "Are these estimates reasonable?" Give students opportunities to say why the estimates are or are not reasonable.

Key Questions

What do you notice about the information on the posters?

What can we learn from this data?

How many responses do we have in all? How do you know?

How does the number of responses compare to the students in our classroom?

How many more . . . ?

How many less . . . ?

Which had the most responses? (Connect the word **mode** to the one that has the most; see Lesson 2.7 for more insights on teaching the term **mode**.)

Part 3: Sorting the Coins (Day 5)

8. Get ready to spill the coins from the counting jar! Gather students in the whole-group area of your classroom, or a space that is large enough to spill out all the coins in the jar. Spread a blanket or something similar on the floor to contain the spillage of coins (see Materials list).

9. Ask students to sit around the edge of the blanket. When students are settled in to a space at the edge of the blanket, place five paper plates or trays on the blanket. Place a label (*half-dollar, quarter, dime, nickel,* and *penny*) in each tray.

10. Explain that you are going to give each student some coins from the jar. Their first task is to sort the coins and place each group in its corresponding tray.

11. Distribute the coins. Observe and note any challenges and successes students may have as they sort their given set of coins.

12. When the coins are sorted, refer back to Poster 1. Were students right in their predictions to the question "What coins are in the jar?" If there is a question about the number of coins in two or more of the groups, you will need to count those coins and compare the groups to know which has more. Encourage students to visually eliminate the groups that don't need to be counted.

Part 4: Totaling the Value of Coins
(Day 5 continued)

13. Before you get started with reflections on Poster 2 (the total value of the coins), remind students of the coin values. Consider asking the key questions shown below.

Part 5: Grouping by Place Value
(Day 5 continued)

14. Display a third poster, flat on the floor, for everyone to see. You will be placing all the coins in piles on this poster so make sure it is big enough. Make three labeled columns on the poster (see Figure 5–3).

Key Questions

How much are half-dollars worth? How many half-dollars make a dollar? Can you put that amount of coins in a stack? Can you make a stack of half-dollars worth one dollar? Stack two half-dollars together to equal one dollar.

How much are quarters worth? How many quarters make a dollar? How many quarters would there be in a stack worth one dollar? Stack four quarters together to equal one dollar.

How much are dimes worth? If you wanted to make a stack of dimes worth one dollar, how many dimes would be in your stack? Stack ten dimes together to equal one dollar.

How much are nickels worth? How many nickels make a dollar? Can you put that amount of coins in a stack? Is a stack of twenty nickels stable enough to stand on its own? Maybe we should find a different way to stack nickels since twenty nickels would make a stack that is too tall and unstable. Do you think we could put the nickels in stacks of two on a ten-frame so we know each completed ten-frame equates to a dollar of nickels?

How much are pennies worth? How many pennies make a dollar? Can you put that amount of coins in a stack? Do you think a stack of one hundred pennies would be too high? Maybe we can find a better way to take care of these coins. Do you think we could put the pennies in stacks of ten on a ten-frame so we know each completed ten-frame equates to a dollar of pennies?

Place-Value Chart

Dollars	Tens	Ones

Figure 5–3. Poster 3 Example

15. Explain to students that they will each be involved in the process of counting the coins and their value. They will use counting cups and ten-frames to help them. Make sure you have these tools readily available.

16. Start by asking, "Who is willing to count the pennies?" Explain that ten pennies should go in each counting cup, then the counting cups should be placed accordingly in each square on a ten-frame. Assign four to six students sitting adjacent to the volunteer to help count pennies. Move the supply of pennies to them. Finally, completed ten-frames should be moved to the place-value chart in the column labeled dollars (as the teacher, you will assist in doing this). Model this process as necessary.

17. Continue asking who is willing to count each coin type including students sitting adjacent to your volunteer until everyone has an assignment.

18. Observe as students count their coins, making note of challenges and successes. As students make dollars, assist in moving the ten-frames and counting cups to the place-value chart. Place the ten-frames and counting cups in rows that make sense for ease in counting them. Combine any partial ten-frames.

**Teaching Insight:
Cups and Ten-Frames as Counting Tools**
Cups and ten-frames are useful tools when counting large quantities of dimes, nickels, and pennies. On the other hand, students should just use cups when counting quarters.

**Teaching Insight:
Including Everyone**
When counting coins (Step 17), group students around the circle, assigning four to six students for each type of coin, making sure each student gets to count some coins. Note that often children will naturally team up if they need a partner.

19. When all that is left is loose change, place those coins on the place-value chart. Do a quick search for missed coins.

20. Tell students that you need help counting. Start with the ones on the place-value chart. If there is a nickel included, ask students if it is possible to trade that nickel for pennies. If there are two nickels, trade them for one dime and place the dime in the tens portions of the place-value chart. Trade coins from a supply other than the counting jar coins. Count the pennies. Record the total value on the place-value chart next to "Ones."

21. Count the tens. This column might have dimes or a combination of coins. If it has the latter, ask students if it would be possible to trade the combinations for dimes. Make the trade, using dimes from a supply other than the counting jar coins. Count the dimes. Record the total value on the place-value chart next to "Tens."

22. Finally, if you haven't already placed coins in rows to group for counting, do that now. Ask students to help you count dollars. Record the total value on the place-value chart next to "Dollars."

23. Refer back to students' estimates (Poster 2). Compare the actual amounts to the estimates.

24. Record the total value of money counted on a strip of paper for everyone to see. Talk about the proper way to write an amount of money (for example, $7.63).

25. Connect the total value to the terms used on the place-value chart. Record this on another strip of paper (for example, for $7.63 the second strip of paper would say "7 Dollars, 6 Tens, and 3 Ones").

26. Set both labels on the rows and piles of coins and take a picture. Print out the picture in an 8-by-10-inch size and display it in the classroom, next to Posters 1 and 2. Encourage students to use these visuals to revisit this counting experience.

27. Have students help you put all coins back in the counting jar. Again, tape the jar shut and place it near the posters and picture of the place-value chart.

Part 6: Introducing and Reading the Book (Day 6)

28. Gather students in the whole-group area of your classroom. Introduce the book *My Rows and Piles of Coins*. Explain that the story takes place in a market in Tanzania. Using a globe, locate Tanzania. Show students where Tanzania is in relation to where they live. Explain that in Tanzania, it is cold in July. In the United States it is warm in July. Briefly tell students that Tanzania is below the equator and it is summer there when it is winter where they live, and winter there when it is summer where they live.

29. Read the book *My Rows and Piles of Coins.* Make sure students can see the illustrations.

> **Teaching Insight:**
> **Picture Books**
> When reading picture books in whole-group settings, consider using a document camera or some form of technology that will project the illustrations for the whole class to more easily see.

Part 7: Discussing Economic Ideas

30. When you are finished reading, ask students if they have ever been to an open-air market. Some of them may have visited craft fairs and/or farmers' markets.

31. Use the above question to segue into the economic ideas in the book; specifically, saving for something special, counting coins, and selling goods. Have a discussion with students about these ideas. Connect Saruni's way of organizing his coins (he puts his coins in piles and rows) to the counting activity students did in previous parts of this lesson. Consider asking the key questions shown here.

Key Questions

Why did we put our coins from the jar in stacks?

Why was Saruni trying to save money?

What did you notice about Saruni's coins?

How are the coins different from our coins? How are they the same? (This is an opportunity to explain that each country has its own special coins; coins from different countries are different than coins from the United States.)

How did Saruni earn money?

What did Saruni do with the money he earned?

Why did Saruni put his coins in rows and piles?

Yeyo, Saruni's mother, earned money by selling goods. What kind of goods did she sell?

How did Saruni's mother, Yeyo, take her goods to market?

Idea$ for Parent$

This is a multiday lesson; with a few modifications you can successfully do it at home with your child. Have your child estimate how much money is in the jar as well as answer the key questions. To encourage the data collection side of this lesson, include friends and relatives in filling out the posters in Part 1. You may want to limit the number of coins in the jar so your child isn't fatigued by all the sorting and counting before he or she reaches the opportunity to use the place-value chart. Read the book in this lesson at home with your child. Encourage discussions about the benefits of earning, saving, and sharing (note that Chapter 6 takes a deeper look at these three concepts).

For further insights on helping your child learn the true value of a dollar via opportunities to earn money, see the section, Additional Ideas for Parents, page 162. See also the Letter to the Parents, page 235.

Pennies for Elephants

A lesson exploring the concept of donations–and the importance of place value for young learners

Overview

Can the children of Boston, with Dorothy and her brother Henry at the helm, raise the six thousand dollars needed to purchase three retired circus elephants for their local zoo? They've only got two months to raise every penny—but every time someone donates—whether it be one cent or one hundred cents—they get their name in the Boston Post newspaper! Based on a true event that took place in 1914, this uplifting story illustrates how a campaign for elephants united the entire city, making cause for celebration and belief in what children can achieve when they work together. In addition to reinforcing how a little bit of money can ultimately add up to a lot, the story introduces yet another answer to the question "How do we earn money?" (in this case the concept of donations—a lot of them!). The story also provides the context for two problem-solving tasks in which students use place-value charts as helpful mathematical tools to total donations. This lesson works best with first and second graders. To continue to explore the idea of donating money versus spending or saving it, see the lessons in Chapter 6.

Mathematics Goal

Students will:
• use place value to add

Literature Connections

Pennies for Elephants by Lita Judge

Time

1 class period

Economics Goals

Students will show:
▶ understanding of the Concept of Money by:
  • identifying that people use money to purchase goods and services
▶ understanding of the Concept of Earning Money by:
  • discussing that work provides income to purchase goods and services

Common Core State Standards for Mathematics:

Number and Operations in Base Ten   1.NBT.2.a.c.4
  • *Understand place value*
  • *Use place value understanding and properties of operations to add and subtract*

Number and Operations in Base Ten   2.NBT.1.a.7
  • *Understand place value*
  • *Use place value understanding and properties of operations to add and subtract*

Materials

Pennies for Elephants Place-Value Chart (Reproducible 5.6), 2 copies per pair of students

a set of 22 dimes and 35 pennies for each pair of students

counting cups (small 1- to 3-ounce cups are ideal), 2 or 3 per pair of students (optional)

Teaching Directions

Part 1: Introducing and Reading the Book

1. Gather students in the whole-group area of your classroom. Before reading the story *Pennies for Elephants*, show students the inside cover to help them understand the setting. The inside cover is illustrated with lifelike newspaper ads from 1914, advertising children's clothing costing less than a dollar and other incredible buys. Young students generally have no information about inflation, so use this opportunity for an explanation about goods costing less. A Studebaker is mentioned in this story. While you are exploring the inside cover with students, you might mention that a Studebaker is a car. Ask your students to tell you how much they think a new car would cost. The ad lists the car for $495. Compare students' estimates to the ad.

2. Read the book, making sure that everyone can see the illustrations.

3. After reading the story, revisit the pages showing illustrations of automobiles and horse-pulled carriages. Ask students to tell what they notice that shows this story takes place a long, long time ago.

Part 2: Exploring Donations and Decimal Points

4. Ask students to recall some of the ways children earned money to buy the elephants. They may offer some of the following ways.

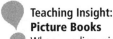

Teaching Insight:
Picture Books
When reading picture books in whole-group settings, consider using a document camera or some form of technology that will project the illustrations for the whole class to more easily see.

Ways Children Earned Money to Buy the Elephants

- hosting a costume party
- hosting a tea party
- ironing handkerchiefs
- running errands
- baking cupcakes and cookies
- selling homemade fudge door-to-door
- washing windows
- playing the violin
- singing in a concert
- putting on a magic show
- washing neighborhood pets

5. Point out that in one case a little boy, Jimmy, donated a nickel he received from the tooth fairy. Ask students to think about the money they get from the tooth fairy. Is it more or less than a nickel? (For more on receiving money from the tooth fairy, see Lesson 2.7, *How Much Money Did the Tooth Fairy Leave?*)

6. In the book, donations are all listed using decimals. Young children are not required to work with decimal points but it makes sense to include a brief explanation since decimals appear in the book. Talk to your students about the especially interesting $.03 donation from three-year-old Anna. Explain that there is a special way to write money amounts if you are going to use a dollar sign and a decimal. The $.03 tells us there are three pennies, no dimes, and no dollars. Make sure your students understand that the dot that looks like the period at the end of the sentence is called a decimal point. Any amounts written to the left of the decimal point are dollars. Point out the $1.14 donation from Henry and Dorothy. If we were using dollars, dimes, and pennies we would know there would be one dollar, one dime, and four pennies.

Part 3: Problem Solving Using Place-Value Charts, Set A

7. Ask students to work with their partners on the next task. Give each pair of students a copy of *Elephants for Pennies* place-value chart (Reproducible 5.6) and a set of pennies and dimes (see Materials list).

> **Teaching Insight:**
> **Sets of Coins**
> Put each set of coins in plastic sandwich bags ahead of time. Include a note in each bag that lists the number of coins that should be in it. Have students count the coins against the list before returning each bag to you at the end of the lesson.

8. Turn to the page in the book with the headline "London Zoo Offers $6,000 on the spot for trained elephants!" Read through the five money amounts listed on the page (referred to as Set A in this section):
    * $.03 from three-year-old Anna
    * $.25 from Anthony (this is his movie money)
    * $.05 from Jimmy (the nickel the tooth fairy left him)
    * $.18 from Frances (to buy part of Tony's ear!)
    * $1.14 from Henry and Dorothy (their life savings)

9. Explain to students that they are going to use their set of coins to find the total value of donations listed on this page. Begin with the three cents given by Anna. Read the line aloud; students need to place three pennies in the Pennies column on their recording sheets.

10. Then read the next line (twenty-five cents from Anthony). Ask students, "What is the least amount of coins you can use to make twenty-five cents when you have only dimes and pennies?" (The least amount is two dimes and five pennies.) Have students place those coins in the Dimes and Pennies columns of their place-value chart.

11. Proceed to Jimmy; Jimmy's nickel is worth five pennies—have students place five pennies on their charts.

12. The fourth donation on the list, Frances' eighteen cents, can be made with one dime and eight pennies. Give students time to place those coins on their charts.

13. Finally, students need to place $1.14—Henry and Dorothy's donation—on their charts.

14. Now ask students to talk with their partner and decide how many dimes should be stacked in the Dollars column of their place-value chart. (You might want to give students small counting cups to hold coins worth a dollar.) Have students place ten dimes in the Dollars column, one dime in the Dimes column, and four pennies in the Pennies column.

15. Look at the coins on students' place-value charts. Ask students if they think they can make any trades. Ask students to count ten pennies and trade for one dime. The dime should be placed in the Dimes column. Ask students if they have more than ten pennies in the Pennies column. They can count ten pennies and trade for another dime.

16. When all possible trades have been made, count the money with students, starting with the dollars. (We have one dollar, six dimes, and five pennies.) The total value is $1.65.

Part 4: Problem Solving Using Place-Value Charts, Set B

17. Turn to the page in the book with the headline: "Brother and Sister, Henry and Dorothy, Earned $.87 hosting Elephant Fund Party!" Read through the five money amounts listed on the page. Display these amounts where everyone can see them (referred to as Set B in this section).
    - $.87 from Henry and Dorothy
    - $.05 from Emily (she ironed handkerchiefs)
    - $.15 from Ethel (she ran errands)
    - $.67 from Walter (he baked and sold cupcakes and cookies)
    - $.48 from Amanda (she sold fudge)

18. Ask students to once again work in pairs, using their set of pennies and dimes to figure out the total value of these five donations. Give students a second copy of Reproducible 5.6 to record how many hundreds, tens, and ones they counted and the total. Tell students that if they have another way to solve this problem, they can use their own strategy; emphasize, however, that they need to record words, pictures, and equations (for example, $.87 + $.05 + $.15 + $.67 + $.48 = $2.22) so you will know how they solved the problem.

Ideas for Parents

You can use this lesson at home with your child just as it is written here; you will need to be your child's discussion and activity partner. Read the book in this lesson at home with your child. Encourage discussions about raising money and getting donations as a form of earning. Use this lesson as an opportunity to connect the traditional way to write money amounts using decimals to actual coins. Use three pennies to connect to $.03. Do the recording of equations but don't expect your child to help you with the addition.

For further insights on helping your child learn the true value of a dollar via opportunities to earn money, see the section, Additional Ideas for Parents, page 162. See also the Letter to the Parents, page 235.

Pennies for Elephants

Place-Value Chart

Name _____   Name _____

How much was donated? Use the place-value chart to help you figure it out!

Dollars (Hundreds)	Dimes (Tens)	Pennies (Ones)

Connecting Money to the Properties of Addition

A lesson in mathematical understandings for young learners

Overview

An important part of understanding the concept of earning money is to understand how it all adds up. This lesson focuses on the mathematical side of the question "How much money is there?" Using sets of coins, students individually complete a grid, making sure that no two coins of the same value are repeated in a row or column. This gamelike element launches students into the next step of writing and solving equations that correspond to the coin values in each row and column of their grids. Students' work reveals interesting connections that form an ideal context for discussing commutative and associative properties. This lesson offers two reproducible recording sheets; use Reproducible 5.7b for younger students who may only be dealing with pennies, nickels, and dimes.

Mathematics Goals

Students will:
- ▶ understand addition as putting together and adding to
- ▶ understand and apply properties of operations
- ▶ use place value understanding and properties of operations to add

Materials

a set of 16 coins (4 quarters, 4 dimes, 4 nickels, and 4 pennies) for every student

Connecting Money to the Properties of Addition sheets (Reproducible 5.7a or 5.7b), 1 copy per student

Common Core State Standards for Mathematics:

Operations and Algebraic Thinking   K.OA.1
- *Understand addition as putting together and adding to, and understand subtraction as taking apart and taking from*

Operations and Algebraic Thinking   1.OA.3.4.5.6.7.8
- *Understand and apply properties of operations and the relationship between addition and subtraction*
- *Add and subtract within 20*
- *Work with addition and subtraction equations*

Number and Operations in Base Ten   2.NBT.5.6.7.9
- *Use place value understanding and properties of operations to add and subtract*

Time

1 class period

Teaching Insight: Sets of Coins

Put each set of coins in plastic sandwich bags ahead of time. Include a note in each bag that lists the number of coins that should be in it. Have students count the coins against the list before returning each bag to you at the end of the lesson.

Teaching Directions

Part 1: Introducing and Completing the Grid

1. Give each student a copy of the recording sheet (Reproducible 5.7a) and a set of sixteen coins (see Materials list).

2. Introduce the grid on the recording sheet to students. Make sure they understand and can differentiate between columns and rows.

3. Read the instructions with students. Explain the task, emphasizing that:
   - students need to place a quarter, dime, nickel, and penny in each row, arranged in any order;
   - each column will have a quarter, dime, nickel, and penny also arranged in any order;
   - there should be a coin placed in each space on the grid;
   - no row will have two or more of the same coins; and
   - no column will have two or more of the same coins.

   For most students, this will be an interesting problem. Some students may have difficulties finding a way to fill the grid without having more than one type of coin in each row and column.

4. Circulate, observing and assisting students as needed until their grids are successfully complete with coins (each student should be working individually on his or her own grid).

Part 2: Writing Equations

5. Direct students' attention to the blanks next to and below their grids. Ask students to fill in the blanks to correspond with the value of coins in each row and column. For example, if the first row of a student's grid has a quarter, dime, nickel, and penny—in that order—the student would write *25* (for quarter), *10* (for dime), *5* (for nickel), and *1* (for penny) in the blanks next to the row.

6. Once students have recorded all the values of the coins on their grids, students complete the equations. Using the example in Step 5, the completed equation would read *25 + 10 + 5 + 1 = 41.*

7. As a final step, students should write a statement answering the question "What did you notice?"

Part 3: Processing the Experience: The Commutative Property

8. Convene students as a whole group. Ask students to volunteer some of the equations they have written. Write the equations where everyone

can see them, forming a list of one equation right under the other.
For example:

$$25 + 1 + 5 + 10 = 41$$
$$10 + 5 + 25 + 1 = 41$$
$$1 + 5 + 10 + 25 = 41$$

9. Ask students, "What do you notice about these equations?" Likely responses are, "The same numbers are in all of the equations but they are in different places in the equations" and "all of the equations total forty-one."

10. Explain to students there is a property called the *commutative property*. This says that when you change the order of addends, it does not change the end result. Because of the commutative property, regardless of the order you put the four numbers in the equations on your recording sheet in, when you add them, you will still end up with a sum of forty-one.

Part 4: Processing the Experience: The Associative Property

11. Next ask students, "Did anyone group numbers within equations to make it easier to add those four numbers?" Expect students to say they added five to twenty-five to make thirty, then added ten, then added one. Another common possibility might be to add ten to twenty-five, then add five, then one. Write those equations where everyone can see them, forming a second list of one equation right under the other. Use parentheses around the numbers students grouped. For example:

$$(25 + 5) + 10 + 1 = 41$$
$$(10 + 25) + 5 + 1 = 41$$

12. Ask students, "What do you notice about these equations?" An example response is, "The same numbers are in all of the equations but the parentheses connect different numbers in the different equations." Once again, students will also probably point out that all of the equations total forty-one.

13. Explain that there is another property for addition called the *associative property*. It is a rule that says when you are adding three or more addends, the sum is the same even if you group different addends.

Part 5: Processing the Experience: Why Doesn't It Work with Subtraction?

14. Finally, explain that the *commutative property* does not work with subtraction. Use $10 - 1$ as an example. Write the equation $10 - 1 = 9$ where everyone can see it. Ask students, "Will you get the same answer if you put the ten and one in the opposite order?" ($1 - 10 = $ _____ and $10 - 1 = $ _____). Emphasize that it is possible to subtract a larger number from a smaller number. If you are dealing with students who are ready to do operations on negative numbers, you could discuss this fact. In this case you're checking to see if you get the same answer

regardless of the order. You do not; the *commutative property* only applies to addition.

Extensions

First-grade students need to have an experience with the associative and commutative properties but are often required to work with only pennies, nickels, and dimes. If your students are in that situation, follow this same lesson but use Reproducible 5.7b, which deals with three types of coins and a 3-by-3 grid. Reproducible 5.7b can also be used for repeated experiences.

Idea$ for Parent$

You can use this lesson at home with your child just as it is written here; you will need to be your child's discussion and activity partner. Use the 3-by-3 grid (Reproducible 5.7b) for younger children and a 4-by-4 grid (Reproducible 5.7a) for older children. The gamelike element provides context for talking about associative and commutative properties. Generally these properties are introduced in first grade.

For further insights on helping your child learn the true value of a dollar via opportunities to earn money, see the section, Additional Ideas for Parents, page 162. See also the Letter to the Parents, page 235.

Connecting Money to the Properties of Addition

Recording Sheet

Name _____   Name _____

Use four quarters, four dimes, four nickels, and four pennies. Place the coins in the grid so each row has one of each type of coin. Place the coins in the grid so each column has one of each type of coin. Record your selections. Write the coin values in the spaces to the right of rows and below the columns. Add the amounts and write the sums. Study your work. Answer the question "What did you notice?"

___ + ___ + ___ + ___ = _____

___ + ___ + ___ + ___ = _____

___ + ___ + ___ + ___ = _____

___ + ___ + ___ + ___ = _____

_____ _____ _____ _____

_____ _____ _____ _____

_____ _____ _____ _____

+_____   +_____   +_____   +_____

_____ _____ _____ _____

What did you notice? _____

_____

_____

Connecting Money to the Properties of Addition

Recording Sheet

Name _____   Name _____

Use three dimes, three nickels, and three pennies. Place the coins in the grid so each row has one of each type of coin. Place the coins in the grid so each column has one of each type of coin. Record your selections. Write the coin values in the spaces to the right of rows and below the columns. Add the amounts and write the sums. Study your work. Answer the question "What did you notice?"

_____ + ___ + ___ = _____

_____ + ___ + ___ = _____

_____ + ___ + ___ = _____

_____ _____ _____

_____ _____ _____

+_____ +_____ +_____

_____ _____ _____

What did you notice? _____

_____

_____

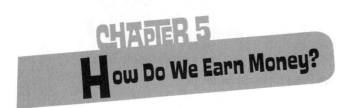

CHAPTER 5
How Do We Earn Money?

Formative Assessment

In this chapter students were asked to collect and represent data, count money, work with place-value concepts, and think about the properties of addition. Students also bumped into the idea of goods and services. As an assessment, ask students to draw or write about goods and services (use Reproducible 5a, *Formative Assessment Activity*). Very young children should limit their lists to two or three things. Second-grade students should be able to go beyond five things. Circulate, observing students while they work.

Children's place-value understanding is fragile. Children need many experiences using place value to build understanding. The best information about a child's understanding of place value comes with individual assessments. Watch students while they count coins with place-value tools. Ask yourself questions such as:

- Are students building an understanding of trading ten pennies for one dime?
- When faced with a number like $.87, do they count eighty-seven pennies or do they know they can use eight dimes?

Note which coins students are able to count. Use the *Formative Assessment Checklist* (Reproducible 5b) to keep a record of students' counting abilities at this stage in the lessons.

Formative Assessment Activity
Chapter 5 Lessons, How Do We Earn Money?

Student Name: _____

Make a list or draw pictures of at least ____ things that are goods and ____ things that are services.

Goods   **Services**

Formative Assessment Checklist
Chapter 5 Lessons, How Do We Earn Money?

Student's Name	Counts Quarters	Counts Quarters and Dimes	Counts Quarters and Nickels	Counts Quarters, Dimes, and Nickels	Counts Quarters and Pennies

From *Why Can't I Have Everything? Teaching Today's Children to Be Financially and Mathematically Savvy, Grades PreK–2* by Jane Crawford.
© 2011 by Scholastic Inc. Permission granted to photocopy for nonprofit use in a classroom or similar place dedicated to face-to-face educational instruction.

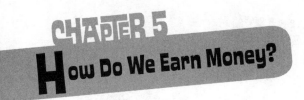

Additional Idea$ for Parent$

Helping Your Child Be Financially Savvy with Earning Money

We all want our children to learn the true value of a dollar. We can explain about the value of money to our children. We can give our children opportunities to deal with money. One of the best ways to help children learn the lesson of the value of a dollar is by allowing them to earn money. Nothing works better than to have children know how hard they have to work to earn money. The end result is children who appreciate the value of money and who learn not to spend it recklessly.

Children who are in the age group targeted by this resource are too young to go door-to-door in the neighborhood (or around their town!) asking for a job. Parents are going to need to be the ones who supply opportunities for very young children to earn money. The chores shown in *Jenny Found a Penny* are appropriate for this age of children. You don't need to pay large sums of money. You do need to pay enough so your child bumps into the idea that there is a balance between earning money and the amount of money you can spend. The goal should be creating a positive work ethic. Your child should have a feeling of accomplishment in addition to getting paid.

Children often have school fundraisers that require selling a good. Unfortunately, parents frequently take their child's order forms to work and/or distribute to relatives to sell for their children, accomplishing the task without involving children. Look at these fundraisers as an opportunity for your child to learn about selling a good. It's not okay for children this age to go door-to-door alone selling something. Go with your child. Talk about the goods and the purpose of the fundraiser so your child has information to share with prospective buyers. Take a supportive role and encourage your child to do the talking when you are at other houses. Jump in and assist any time it appears your child needs help.

CHAPTER 6

Should We Spend, Save, or Share?

Emphasize the Value of Sharing—and Making Decisions on Whether to Spend, Save, or Share in Good or Bad Financial Times

Overview

In our world today it is ever more important to teach children not only the consequences of spending and the benefits of saving, but also the value of sharing. The lessons in this chapter aim to help children explore and understand all three: spending, saving, and sharing.

Lessons 6.1 and **6.2** immerse students in gorgeous multicultural stories that address surviving hard financial times, working together, setting goals, and sharing. Students make decisions about spending and saving money, as well as revisit the idea of goods versus services.

In **Lesson 6.3** students add to or subtract pennies from their ten-frames to show quantity. The game reinforces the fact that a big part of knowing how to spend or save is knowing how to add and subtract! **Lesson 6.4** provides a gamelike context for further enforcing students' financial and mathematical skills. **Lesson 6.5** gives students focused experiences in using quarters as landmarks in adding and subtracting. Last but not least, **Lesson 6.6** gives students the unique opportunity to act out money-sharing problems.

Mathematically these lessons continue in building opportunities for students to collect, interpret, and represent data; decompose numbers; and bump into place-value concepts.

For additional lessons emphasizing the importance of sharing money—specifically what children can achieve through generosity—see Lessons 5.5, *My Rows and Piles of Money*, and 5.6, *Pennies for Elephants*.

The Lessons

Formative Assessment 189

Formative Assessment Checklist 190

Literature Used in This Chapter

A Chair for My Mother by Vera B. Williams

Chicken Sunday by Patricia Polacco

Benny's Pennies by Pat Brisson

Additional Idea$ for Parent$

A Chair for My Mother

An economics and mathematics lesson focused on the value of sharing and saving for young learners

Overview

This lesson gives students the opportunity to make their own decisions in regards to the question "Should we spend, save, or share?" The lesson opens with the Reading Rainbow book *A Chair for My Mother*—an all-time favorite story that has received various awards, including the Caldecott Honor. Students in turn think about jobs they could do to earn money. They then decide what portion of the money they would spend and what portion they would save. Students create posters representing their decisions via illustrations and mathematical equations. In a whole-group discussion, students compare and contrast the amounts of money they've decided to spend and save, ultimately categorizing their posters by *more savings*, *equal savings and spending*, and *more spending*.

Common Core State Standards for Mathematics:

Counting and Cardinality   K.CC.6.7
- *Compare numbers*

Operations and Algebraic Thinking   1.OA.1.7
- *Represent and solve problems involving addition and subtraction*
- *Work with addition and subtraction equations*

Measurement and Data   1.MD.4
- *Represent and interpret data*

Operations and Algebraic Thinking   2.OA.1.3
- *Represent and solve problems involving addition and subtraction*
- *Work with equal groups of objects to gain foundations for multiplication*

Measurement and Data   2.MD.8
- *Work with time and money*

Mathematics Goals

Students will:
- ▶ compare numbers
- ▶ represent and solve problems
- ▶ compose and decompose numbers
- ▶ work with addition equations
- ▶ represent and interpret data
- ▶ decide if a number is odd or even
- ▶ solve problems involving money

Economics Goals

Students will show:
- ▶ understanding of the Concept of Earning Money by:
  - • discussing the requirements of various jobs
- ▶ understanding of the Concept of Goods and Services by:
  - • discussing that people save money for future goods and services

Literature Connections

A Chair for My Mother by Vera B. Williams

Materials

chart paper or some means of displaying written lists for students to see

9-by-18-inch white construction paper, 1 sheet per student

markers

measurement cubes

Time

1 class period

Teaching Directions

Part 1: Introducing and Reading the Book

1. Gather students in the whole-group area of your classroom. Show them the cover of the book *A Chair for My Mother*. What do they see? Point out to students that the little girl at the door is Rosa and the woman inside is her mother. Ask, "What do you think Rosa's mother is doing?" It is likely that a student will say she works there. Tell students you'll read the story together to discover what's happening.

2. Read *A Chair for My Mother* to your students, making sure they can see the illustrations.

Part 2: Discussing the Book

3. After you've read the book through once, ask students key questions, Set 1.

Part 3: Deciding the Monetary Value of a Job

4. With students, brainstorm jobs that they could do. Make a list of the jobs for everyone to see (consider using chart paper).

5. Explain that you'd like to assign each job a value (pay) that is less than one dollar. Ask students, "Which job should pay the most?" Listen while students explain which job deserves to have the most pay. Compare the responsibilities of each job; talk about the challenges of each job. Write the decided value of each job next to it on the list. For example, students might suggest helping to set the table and/or walking the dog as jobs. They might decide that walking the dog is more fun and is easier than setting the table. Setting the table may receive a value of seventy cents whereas walking the dog pays only fifty cents. Direct the conversation to skills required and efforts made in accomplishing different jobs, which is why some jobs pay more, see key questions, Set 2.

Part 4: Deciding How Much to Spend and Save

6. Have students work at tables. Give each student a 9-by-18-inch sheet of white construction paper and markers. Explain that each of them will be making a poster. Students can follow the poster instructions on page 168.

**Teaching Insight:
About the Book**

In the story, Rosa's family loses all their furniture in a house fire. Rosa, her mother, and her grandmother diligently work to save money to replace it—their goal being the purchase of a sofa chair for Rosa's overworked mom. The story reinforces the value of sharing and saving money—especially in financially hard times.

**Teaching Insight:
Picture Books**

When reading picture books in whole-group settings, consider using a document camera or some form of technology that will project the illustrations for the whole class to more easily see.

Key Questions

Set 1

Where did the characters in this book put their coins?

Why did they do that?

How did they get their money?

Key Questions

Set 2

Which job should pay the most? Why?

Which job should pay the least? Why?

Which job has the most responsibilities? Explain.

Which job has the most challenges? Explain.

Poster Instructions

a. Divide the paper into top and bottom sections.

b. At the top, write one of the jobs from the list and the corresponding amount of money it pays; write the amount with a cents sign.

c. At the top, draw which coins make that amount of money.

d. At the bottom, draw two illustrations: a pocket and a jar. The pocket is for money students would spend, and the jar is for money they would save (based on what they earn in the job). These drawings need to be large enough for students to draw coins inside of them.

e. Draw the corresponding coins in the pocket and the jar.

f. At the bottom, write an equation for each group of coins.

Teaching Insight:
Deciding What to Spend and Save
Note that for Step c, one student may draw fifty cents as two quarters, whereas another may draw it as five dimes. This will likely influence how they divide their money into savings and spending—the two quarters division will usually end up with a quick even split, whereas the five dimes will end up with a more drawn-out decision about dividing the fifty cents between the two choices. Be sure to tell students that the amounts in the pocket and jar don't have to be equal (of course, if the job they choose has a value that is an odd number, they cannot divide the number equally). Students may decide to divide by the number of coins, disregarding values. They may also choose to either spend more or save more; either way is fine for the purpose of this lesson. How children do the task gives insight to their thinking—are they spenders or are they savers?

Teaching Insight:
Understanding the Idea of Odd Numbers
If your students have not bumped into the idea of odd numbers, take a few minutes to represent numbers by matching measurement cubes (or pennies) in pairs. Help students become aware of the fact that even numbers always are a pair, whereas odd numbers never can be built as pairs. As you pair the number of objects from 1 to 20, record which are even numbers and which are odd numbers. Ask students to look at your list and see if they notice a pattern. Point out that numbers ending in 0, 2, 4, 6, and 8 are even numbers. Numbers ending in 1, 3, 5, 7 and 9 are odd numbers. You will probably need to revisit the idea of odd and even numbers again, always connecting the physical with the number sequence.

Part 5: Processing and Comparing

7. When students have completed their posters, reconvene as a whole group. Select students to show their posters and explain what job they chose, how much they will earn, and how they divided their savings and spending money.

8. Ask students to compare the value of the coins in the pocket and the value of the coins in the jar on their posters. Ask students to use the symbols $<$, $>$, and $=$ to compare those amounts. Students should write the two numbers with the correct symbol on the bottom of their posters.

9. Designate a place in the classroom for students to display their posters. Consider using the board. Create and post three labels in the display space: *More savings, Equal savings and spending*, and *More spending*. Ask students to decide which label their poster should go under. Help them think through the idea that if they put more money in their picture of the jar, they were saving more money. If they put more money in their pocket, they were spending more money. Help students display their posters in the correct category.

10. When all posters are displayed, ask key questions.

Extensions

As an extension, raise the amount earned from being less than one dollar to being exactly one dollar. Students need to divide their dollar three ways: some for saving, some for spending, and some for sharing (supporting a cause or giving to a charity). Ask students to complete another poster showing the division of one dollar three ways. Also see Lesson 5.5, *My Rows and Piles of Coins*, for another literature connection on saving and sharing money.

Ideas for Parents

You can use this lesson at home with your child just as it is written here; you will need to be your child's discussion and activity partner. Read the book in this lesson at home with your child. Encourage discussions about spending, saving, and sharing money. Brainstorm a list of jobs. When your child has completed his or her poster, display it in your home; refer to it from time to time as you work through other lessons. Keep in mind that this lesson is about giving children a context for beginning to divide money, rather than a product of what happens when you divide; when your child divides money, don't be concerned that the division isn't equal. The younger the child, the more likely the division will be based on the number of coins. Young children will likely put one coin in the pocket and the next in the jar without consideration of coin value.

For further insights on helping your child learn the value of sharing money via charity and gifts, see the section, Additional Ideas for Parents, page 191. See also the Letter to the Parents, page 236.

A Hat for Miss Eula

A data collection lesson involving further exploration of sharing and saving money for young learners

Overview

This lesson builds on children's understandings from Lesson 6.1, this time involving a cast of delightful characters in the award-winning book *Chicken Sunday* (an ALA Notable Book, Booklist Editor's Choice, and IRA/CBC Children's Choice Book). Woven with valuable cultural as well as financial lessons, the story provides the context for revisiting the concept of goods versus services (first introduced in Chapter 5). Students then collect, represent, and interpret personal data on what they think the children have done and will do with their money, in the light of Mr. Kodinski giving them the hat.

Common Core State Standards for Mathematics:

Counting and Cardinality   K.CC.5.6.7
- *Count to tell the number of objects*
- *Compare numbers*

Measurement and Data   K.MD.3
- *Classify objects and count the number of objects in each category*

Measurement and Data   1.MD.4
- *Represent and interpret data*

Measurement and Data   2.MD.10
- *Represent and interpret data*

Mathematics Goal

Students will:
▶ solve simple compare problems involving information from graphs

Economics Goals

Students will show:
▶ understanding of the Concept of Money by:
 •identifying that people use money to purchase goods and services
▶ understanding of the Concept of Goods and Services by:
 •identifying examples of goods and services
 •discussing that people save money for future goods and services

Literature Connections

Chicken Sunday by Patricia Polacco

Materials

1 piece of tag board or laminated colored construction paper (can be the same materials used in Lesson 2.1)

clothespins, 1 per student

Time

30 minutes

Teaching Directions

Part 1: Introducing and Reading the Book

1. Gather students in the whole-group area of your classroom. Show them the cover of the book *Chicken Sunday*. Talk about the characters on the front cover. Ask, "How do you think these three children feel about Miss Eula?"

2. Read *Chicken Sunday* to your students, making sure they can see the illustrations.

Part 2: Discussing the Book

3. Explain and talk about some of the cultural ideas in the book. Give students background information on the author Patricia Polacco; she has family roots in Ukraine and Russia. She grew up hearing stories and interacting with older family members. She has friends who are African American with family roots in the bayous of Louisiana, and she also spends time with their families and listens to their stories. Babushka is a name for a grandmother. Ask students, "Is there a name you call your grandmother by?" On the page introducing the idea of "Chicken Sundays," point out the actual pictures within the drawing. These are family pictures from the author's friends' family.

Part 3: Revisiting the Concept of Goods and Services

4. In the story, the children think about asking the hat shop owner if they can sweep his shop to earn money. Ask your students, "Would sweeping the shop by a *good* or a *service*?" Ask them to explain how they know it would be a service.

5. Turn to the part of the story where the children are using wax and dye to make a special kind of colored egg. Explain that those eggs originally were made in Russia. Mr. Kodinski calls them Pysanky eggs and tells the children he hasn't seen any of those since he left Russia. (This might be a good time to locate Russia on a map or a globe and see how far it is from where your students live.)

6. Ask your students, "How does Mr. Kodinski help the children earn money?" Ask your students, "Are the Pysanky eggs the children decorated a good or a service?" Let students explain why the eggs are a good that the children sell. Also, ask your students, "Do you think the eggs will all sell for the exact price? Why or why not?" This might be a good time to discuss that if goods are extra special in some way, they sometimes cost more.

Teaching Insight:
Picture Books
When reading picture books in whole-group settings, consider using a document camera or some form of technology that will project the illustrations for the whole class to more easily see.

Teaching Insight:
About the Book
Miss Eula, known for cooking up a sumptuous fried chicken dinner, wishes to have one of the elegant hats from Mr. Kodinski's shop. The children in her neighborhood make note of Miss Eula's wish and hope to buy her one. They decide to approach Mr. Kodinski to see if they can sweep his shop for money; when they get to his shop they witness an act of racism on the hat shop; Mr. Kodinski sees them and mistakenly accuses them of vandalizing his shop. To prove their innocence, the children hand-dye eggs in the folk-art style that Patricia's grandmother had taught her, then present them to the merchant. Moved by the remembrance of his homeland, Mr. Kodinski, a Holocaust survivor, encourages the children to sell the "Pysanky" eggs in his shop. He then gives them a hat, which Miss Eula proudly wears on Easter Sunday.

7. Finally, ask students the last three questions from the key questions list, Set 1.

Part 4: Collecting Data

8. Using tag board or laminated construction paper, create a graph with two columns: *Saved it for something special* and *Spent it on something like candy*. Tell students, "We are going to do some quick data collection." Give each student a clothespin; explain to students that they will be answering a question by clipping their clothespin to the side of the tag board that matches their response.

9. Ask them the key question, "What do you think the children did with the money they earned selling eggs?" Have students clip their clothespins to the side of the graph that corresponds with their opinion of what the children did with the money.

10. When all students have finished attaching their clothespins, ask key questions, Set 2.

11. As closure, give students the opportunity to talk about gifts they have given to someone special in their lives.

Ideas for Parents

With a few modifications you can successfully use this lesson outside of the classroom. Read the book in this lesson at home with your child. Encourage discussions about the cultural and financial ideas in the book. Rather than collect data (which is challenging with only one child to survey!), simply ask the question and proceed with the other steps.

For further insights on helping your child learn the value of sharing money via charity and gifts, see the section, Additional Ideas for Parents, page 191. See also the Letter to the Parents, page 236.

Key Questions

Set 1

Would sweeping the shop be a good or a service? Explain.

How does Mr. Kodinski help the children earn money?

Are the Pysanky eggs the children decorated a good or a service? Explain.

Do you think the eggs will all sell for the exact price? Why or why not?

What do the children plan to do with their money?

What happened that made them not have to spend it?

What do you think the children did with the money they earned selling eggs?

Key Questions

Set 2

What do you notice about our data?

Which has more?

Which has less?

Do you think this reflects what you would do with the money?

Benny's Pennies

A lesson on sharing, including a ten-frame game for young learners

Overview

Continuing the discussion of whether to spend, save, or share (and instilling the power of giving in children), *Benny's Pennies* is a sweet story about a boy who spends his five pennies on gifts for others—from his mom to his brother to even the family dog. The story provides the financial context for a ten-frame game in which students get their turn at managing Benny's pennies. They add to or subtract pennies from their ten-frames to show quantity, then work with addition and subtraction equations. The game reinforces the fact that a big part of knowing how to spend or save is knowing how to add and subtract! Consider repeated experiences with the lesson in independent and/or small-group stations. This lesson is most appropriate for children learning about counting and counting on. See the "Formative Assessment" section, page 189, for further support in assessing using this lesson.

Mathematics Goals

Students will:
▶ count and compare numbers
▶ add to or subtract pennies to show a quantity
▶ work with addition and subtraction equations

Common Core State Standards for Mathematics:

Counting and Cardinality   K.CC.2.3.4.a.b.c.5.6
- *Know number names and the count sequence*
- *Count to tell the number of objects*
- *Compare numbers*

Operations and Algebraic Thinking   K.OA.2.3
- *Understand addition as putting together and adding to, and understand subtraction as taking apart and taking from*

Operations and Algebraic Thinking   1.OA.1.6.7.8
- *Represent and solve problems involving addition and subtraction*
- *Add and subtract within 20*
- *Work with addition and subtraction equations*

Economics Goals

Students will show:
▶ understanding of the Concept of Goods and Services by:
 • identifying that people are buyers and sellers of goods and services

Materials

a set of 6 to 10 pennies for each student

Ten-Frame (Reproducible 3.3), 1 copy per student

1 die (ideally a large classroom die)

Spinner (Reproducible 6.3), assembled

Literature Connections

Benny's Pennies by Pat Brisson

Time

1 class period

Teaching Directions

Part 1: Introducing and Reading the Book

1. Gather students in the whole-group area of your classroom. Before you begin reading *Benny's Pennies*, ask students to think about and share the times when they have given someone a present.

2. Read *Benny's Pennies* to your students, making sure they can see the illustrations.

Part 2: Discussing the Book

3. Ask students to retell how Benny spent his pennies. Did he buy something for himself or did he share?

Part 3: Playing the Game

4. Let students know that they will now have a turn with Benny's pennies. For very young children, give each student six pennies and a ten-frame (Reproducible 3.3). Explain that you will roll the die. You will call out the number rolled. The number you call out is the number of pennies that each student should place on her or his ten-frame.

5. Play the game. Encourage students to use information to build on and remove from each time a new number is called in order to reinforce the concepts of addition and subtraction. Push for students to count on and count back rather than count all. Ask key questions and connect students' work to equations; for example, when you spin a number 7, ask the key questions.

Teaching Insight:
Picture Books
When reading picture books in whole-group settings, consider using a document camera or some form of technology that will project the illustrations for the whole class to more easily see.

Teaching Insight:
Sets of Coins
Put each set of coins in plastic sandwich bags ahead of time. Include a note in each bag that lists the number of coins that should be in it. Have students count the coins against the list before returning each bag to you at the end of the lesson.

Teaching Insight:
For Students with More Experiences Counting
For students with more experiences counting, give each student ten pennies and a ten-frame (Reproducible 3.3). Instead of the die, use the *Spinner* sheet (Reproducible 6.3). Explain that you will spin the spinner and call out the number. Students place the corresponding number of pennies on their ten-frames. Repeat, spinning and calling out another number.

Teaching Insight:
Counting On
Recording equations works for children with more advanced counting skills. Some children stop and recount everything. This is about maturity and skill. The ability to know where the counting begins and count on from that number is important. If there are three pennies on the ten-frame and two are added, many children will count "one, two, three, four, five." We need children to just say "three" and count on "four, five" afterward.

Key Questions

How did you build your seven? (*Record student responses like 5 + 2 = 7 and 4 + 3 = 7 where everyone can see.*)

How many more would you need to make ten? (*Record responses both as 10 − __ = 7 and 7 + __ = 10.*)

6. As students play, also watch and record the answers to the formative assessment questions.

Formative Assessment Questions

Which students have difficulties counting these quantities?

Which students clear the ten-frame each time?

Which students use the previous number and remove or add to it to build numbers?

Which students use ten-frame knowledge to make a number (for example, when the number 5 is rolled, a student just fills one side of the ten-frame without counting the pennies)?

Teaching Insight:
Individual Assessments
You may want to assess students privately to determine if they are able to add to and remove from to make a quantity of pennies. You may discover that they understand they can build numbers using the information they already have, but just have developed the habit of clearing their ten-frame each time.

Extensions

This lesson can be used as an independent or small-group activity. Ask students to spin, place the corresponding number of pennies on their ten-frames, and record equations.

Ideas for Parents

You can use this lesson at home with your child just as it is written here; you will need to be your child's discussion and activity partner (spin the spinner, ask questions, etc.). Read the book in this lesson at home with your child. Encourage discussions about the concept of giving gifts. When placing pennies on the ten-frame, if your child tends to count all instead of count on, repeat this lesson on other days to help reinforce and give opportunities for counting on.

For further insights on helping your child learn the value of sharing money via charity and gifts, see the section, Additional Ideas for Parents, page 191. See also the Letter to the Parents, page 236.

Spinner

Instructions for assembling the spinner:

1. Copy the spinner onto durable paper (ideally, card stock). Also have an 8½ by-11-inch sheet of the same paper on hand to mount the spinner on (this will be the base).

2. Cut out the spinner circle.

3. Punch a hole in the center of the spinner.

4. Punch a hole somewhere near the center of the base.

5. Use a ruler to draw a straight line from the center of the base to one of the corners.

6. Cut a small section of plastic straw (approximately ¼ inch) to use as a washer.

7. Put a bent paper clip through the base.

8. Place the section of plastic straw on the paper clip.

9. Place the spinner on the paper clip, over the straw.

10. Bend the top of the paper clip and tape it to keep the spinner from flying off.

11. Place tape on the bottom to hold the paper clip to the base.

12. Spin. The line points to the winning space.

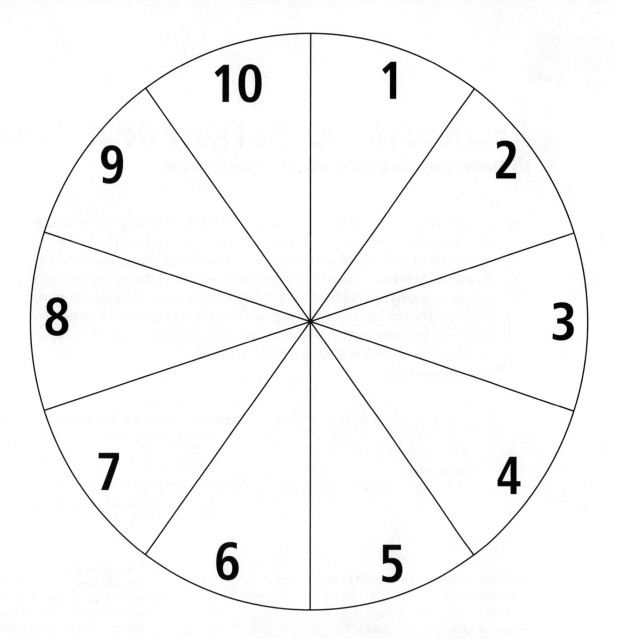

From *Why Can't I Have Everything? Teaching Today's Children to Be Financially and Mathematically Savvy, Grades PreK–2* by Jane Crawford. © 2011 by Scholastic Inc. Permission granted to photocopy for nonprofit use in a classroom or similar place dedicated to face-to-face educational instruction.

How Much Money Do I Have Now? Game

A lesson in understanding place value, adding, and subtracting

Overview

A significant part of spending, saving, and sharing money is knowing how to manage the corresponding transactions. This lesson provides a gamelike context for further enforcing students' financial and mathematical skills. In small groups, students roll a die and add or remove coins on their game boards accordingly. Sometimes their move will require trading coins with another player to have the sufficient coin(s) and value. The player who correctly fills his or her game board first is considered the winner. The game takes luck and counting skills to win, and gives children a reason for trading and counting coins. All children at all ages can play this game.

Mathematics Goal

Students will:

▶ build an understanding of place value

Common Core State Standards for Mathematics:

Number and Operations in Base Ten   1.NBT.2.a.b.c.4
- *Understand place value*
- *Use place value understanding and properties of operations to add and subtract*

Number and Operations in Base Ten   2.NBT.1.a.8
- *Understand place value*
- *Use place value understanding and properties of operations to add and subtract*

Materials

a set of 10 dimes and 10 pennies per player

die with sides labeled: *+10, +10, −10, +1, +1, −1, 1* per small group of players

Game Directions (Reproducible 6.4a), 1 copy per player

Game Board (Reproducible 6.4b), 1 copy per player

Teaching Insight: Sets of Coins

Put each set of coins in plastic sandwich bags ahead of time. Include a note in each bag that lists the number of coins that should be in it. Have students count the coins against the list before returning each bag to you at the end of the lesson.

Time

1 class period

Teaching Directions

Part 1: Introducing the Game

1. Explain to students that they are going to play a game in small groups. Emphasize that they will only be using dimes and pennies. Show students the game board (Reproducible 6.4a) and the die.

2. Ask students, "Which coin would you add to your game board if you rolled a +10?" (Students should respond "dime!") Then ask students, "Which coin would you add to your game board if you rolled a +1?" (Students should respond "penny!")

3. Ask students, "What do you think you should do if there is a minus sign in front of the number?" Make sure students understand that they add a coin if there is a plus sign and remove a coin if there is a minus sign. If the number is "10" it is a dime. If the number is "1" it is a penny.

> 💡 **Teaching Insight:**
> **Creating the Die**
> To make the die for this game, use small blocks, number cubes, or large-sized dice. For the labels, use white ¾-inch round stickers. Label sides with +10, +10, −10, +1, +1, and −1.

Part 2: Modeling the Game

4. Explain how to play the game by displaying a copy of the game board for everyone to see (options include using a document camera or overhead projector). Roll the die and model adding or removing the corresponding coins. As you demonstrate and roll, ask students, "How much money do I have now?"

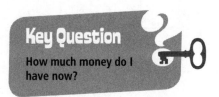

Key Question

How much money do I have now?

5. Continue to play until you have an opportunity to demonstrate a trade. If a student rolls a −10 and does not have at least one dime or ten pennies, no coins are removed. If a student rolls a −1 and has dimes but no pennies, a trade must be made before the coin can be removed. A student making a trade might say, "I am trading one dime for ten pennies." Stress the importance of having the other players watch the trade being made to make sure that the correct coins are traded.

6. Explain that the winner of the game is the player who fills his or her game board completely with dimes in the spaces labeled *Dime* and pennies in the spaces labeled *Penny*, plus returns extra coins to the coin supply. Clarify that students might have more than ten dimes and ten pennies at the end. There is no require-ment to exactly fill the game board to win.

Part 3: Playing the Game

7. Ask if there are any questions. Give each student a copy of the game directions and the game board (Reproducibles 6.4a and 6.4b). Have students play in small groups of two or three. Circulate, observing students and noting any particular challenges and successes. Especially note if you observe a student having dif-ficulties making trades because she or he is uncertain about the values of dimes.

Idea$ for Parent$

You can use this lesson at home with your child just as it is written here; consider gathering other family members to create a team of players for the game. Use Reproducible 6.4a as a quick reference to the game's directions. Take the lead in helping to count and trade coins if your child is young.

For further insights on helping your child learn the value of sharing money via charity and gifts, see the section, Additional Ideas for Parents, page 191. See also the Letter to the Parents, page 236.

How Much Money Do I Have Now?

Game Directions

You'll need:

1 game board per player (Reproducible 6.4b)

a set of 10 dimes and 10 pennies per player

1 die with sides labeled: 110, 110, 210, 11, 11, 21

Directions

1. Players take turns rolling the die:

    a. If a player rolls 110, or 210, the player adds or removes a dime from his or her game board, then hands the die to the next player.

    b. If a player rolls a 11, or 21, the player adds or removes a penny from his or her game board, then hands the die to the next player.

    c. If a player has no pennies or dimes and rolls a 21 or 210, coins can obviously not be removed. That player's turn is done; she or he hands the die to the next player.

    d. If a player has no dimes and fewer than ten pennies and rolls a 210, no coins are removed. That player's turn is done; she or he hands the die to the next player.

    e. If a player does not have the appropriate coin(s) to correspond to the number rolled, but does have coins, the player will need to do a coin trade. For example, when a player has the Penny spaces completed and needs to trade for a dime, the player should say, "I am trading ten pennies for one dime." Players check each other's trades and agree before the die is handed to the next player.

2. Before completing his or her turn, the player should answer the question, "How much money do I have now?"

3. The winner of this game is the first player who:

    • Fills her or his game board completely with dimes in the spaces labeled Dime and pennies in the spaces labeled Penny.

    • Returns extra coins to the coin supply. (There is no requirement to exactly fill the game board to win.)

How Much Money Do I Have Now?

Game Board

Tens		Ones	
Dime	Dime	Penny	Penny
Dime	Dime	Penny	Penny
Dime	Dime	Penny	Penny
Dime	Dime	Penny	Penny
Dime	Dime	Penny	Penny

Using Quarters for Landmarks
A lesson in counting and counting on for young learners

Overview

In this lesson students solve addition and subtraction problems that use the quarter as a landmark. In the United States, quarters are a landmark in counting coins. Many students have had quarter experiences by the time they get to first grade. It is useful for your students to simply know that one quarter is worth twenty-five cents, two quarters are worth fifty cents, three quarters are worth seventy-five cents, and four quarters are worth a dollar. There isn't as much learning value in being able to use a traditional way of adding two-digit numbers, such as $25 + 25 = 50$, as there is for students to simply be able to say "Two quarters equal fifty cents." This is a lesson for students who count by fives and tens and have had some experience in counting on by tens and fives. Most second-grade students and some first-grade students will be able to participate in this lesson. See the "Formative Assessment" section, page 189, for further support in assessing using this lesson.

Mathematics Goals

Students will:

▶ add or subtract ten from a number
▶ count on from a number
▶ use addition and subtraction to solve problems
▶ use place value understanding to add and subtract

Economics Goals

Students will show:

▶ understanding of the Concept of Money by:
   • recognizing various forms of U.S. currency

Common Core State Standards for Mathematics:

Number and Operations in Base Ten   1.NBT.1.4.5
• *Extend the counting sequence*
• *Understand place value*
• *Use place value understanding and properties of operations to add and subtract*

Operations and Algebraic Thinking   2.OA.1
• *Represent and solve problems involving addition and subtraction*

Number and Operations in Base Ten   2.NBT.2.5.8.9
• *Understand place value*
• *Use place value understanding and properties of operations to add and subtract*

Materials

3 quarters for each group of two to four students

a set of coins (1 penny, 3 nickels, 1 dime, 4 quarters) for each group of two to four students

0–99 pocket chart

Time

1 class period

Teaching Insight:
Sets of Coins

Put each set of coins in plastic sandwich bags ahead of time. Include a note in each bag that lists the number of coins that should be in it. Have students count the coins against the list before returning each bag to you at the end of the lesson.

Teaching Directions

Part 1: Counting Quarters

1. Have students work in small groups of two to four. Give each group three quarters. Move around the classroom, counting and recounting the quarters so students hear the melody of the counting words, "twenty-five, fifty, seventy-five, a dollar." Your goal in this first step is to help students be able to rote count by twenty-fives—a useful skill.

Part 2: Counting Using Quarters as Landmarks

2. Now give each group of students a set of coins (see Materials list). Ask students to first focus on one quarter and one dime. Model counting these coins for students, saying, "Twenty-five, thirty-five."

3. Next ask students to use two quarters and one dime. Model counting for students, saying, "Twenty-five, fifty, sixty." Reinforce the idea that you count the coins with the most value first.

Part 3: Solving Addition Problems

4. Ask the key questions on page 185 that prompt the students to think about adding coins to landmark quarter amounts, giving students time to build the corresponding amounts with their sets of coins. After each question, have students explain how they thought about solving the problem. Ask students to count coins for you. End each question by asking students to count the coins with you. While you are questioning, encourage students to share their thoughts with a partner before answering in a whole-group setting. Encourage students to think about amounts mentally but allow them to use paper if they want to. Listen while students explain how they figured out the answer to the question.

Part 4: Solving Subtraction Problems

5. After asking questions in which students add a coin to landmark quarter amounts, ask students to subtract. For most students, thinking about an amount less than a quarter will be more a mental task than a coin-counting task.

Teaching Insight:
Using a Hundreds Chart
Your students may have had experience with a 0–99 chart, adding ten to a number. If they have, you can refer back to that chart and show that ten more than twenty-five is thirty-five; for Step 3, refer to the chart to show that ten more than fifty is sixty.

Teaching Insight:
Counting Coins
The process in Step 4 may seem redundant; however, hearing the words and being able to remember the melody of the number sequence helps students count on when they are required to switch from counting by twenty-fives to counting by tens or fives or ones. Many of your students may easily count on from a number with a different sequence. For those students who are struggling to work through this, having another experience will be useful.

Part 5: Processing the Experience

6. Ask students if they thought about the corresponding coin when they added ten cents (dime), five cents (nickel), and fifteen cents (dime and nickel). Discuss if it is easier to think about the amount using dimes or nickels. Expect some students to say they thought of pennies and counted up or down from a number.

7. Explain that twenty-five, fifty, and seventy-five are landmark numbers when it comes to counting money. If you are making change or getting change from a dollar, it is likely change will be made with quarters. Quarters allow a person to give the fewest coins when making change from a dollar.

Idea$ for Parent$

You can use this lesson at home with your child just as it is written here; you will need to be your child's discussion and activity partner. This lesson is likely too difficult if your child is not able to count on and skip count (for example, count by fives). However, do complete the first step in this lesson, involving counting by quarters. This is a rote counting sequence, which means your child will hear and learn the melody of the words *twenty-five, fifty, seventy-five, one hundred.* That is a useful skill, though it is never tested at kindergarten level.

For further insights on helping your child learn the value of sharing money via charity and gifts, see the section, Additional Ideas for Parents, page 191. See also the Letter to the Parents, page 236.

Teaching Insight:
Using the Hundreds Chart
You may want to refer back to the 0–99 chart while you talk about the subtraction problems. It is likely that ten less will be easier for students to see than five less.

Key Questions

Adding Coins to Landmark Quarter Amounts

How much would you have if you had ten cents more than a quarter? two quarters? three quarters? *(Count this both with dimes and with nickels.)*

How much would you have if you had five cents more than a quarter? two quarters? three quarters?

How much would you have if you had fifteen cents more than a quarter? two quarters? three quarters? *(Depending on students' experience, you may want students to count this with only nickels or with dimes and nickels.)*

How much would you have if you had one cent more than a quarter? two quarters? three quarters?

Key Questions

Subtracting Coins from Landmark Quarter Amounts

How much would you have if you had ten cents less than a quarter? two quarters? three quarters?

How much would you have if you had one cent less than a quarter? two quarters? three quarters?

How much would you have if you had five cents less than a quarter? two quarters? three quarters?

Acting Out Money-Sharing Problems

A lesson in sharing money for young learners

Overview

In this engaging lesson, students assume the roles of actors and actresses in money transactions. Students who are not acting have an important role as audience members, solving the problem presented by the actors. Acting out story problems helps young students further build their financial and mathematical understanding. Consider doing one or two of these problems every day, giving every student the opportunity to take part in acting out a problem.

Common Core State Standards for Mathematics:

Counting and Cardinality   K.CC.5
* *Count to tell the number of objects*

Operations and Algebraic Thinking   K.OA.1.2.3.4.5
* *Understand addition as putting together and adding to, and understand subtraction as taking apart and taking from*

Mathematics Goals

Students will:
▶ count to tell how many
▶ put numbers together to add and take numbers apart to subtract

Economics Goals

Students will show:
▶ understanding of the Concept of Money by:
  • recognizing various forms of U.S. currency

Time

20 minutes

Materials

20 pennies

Teaching Directions

Introducing the Lesson

1. Gather students in the whole-group area of your classroom. Explain to students that they will be acting out problems about sharing money.

Acting Out the Problem

2. Select a problem from the Money-Sharing Problems list on page 188. Request volunteers to act out the problem. Hand out pennies to the actors as appropriate for the problem. Ask students in the audience to take on the role of problem solvers. The actors do what the problems describe and the audience solves the problem.

3. Observe and provide support as the problem is acted out and the audience solves it. Check to make sure that the students' thinking is accurate. Encourage discussion about the quantities of coins.

4. As students solve each problem, record corresponding equations for everyone to see. Help students make the connections. Be sure to note when you use a plus or a minus sign so students become aware of the two operations.

Extensions

As an extension, have students work individually, in partners, or small groups to create their own money-sharing problems.

Teaching Insight:
Personalizing the Problems
Instead of using the names in the problems, replace them with actual names of your students.

Idea$ for Parent$

With a few modifications you can successfully use this lesson outside of the classroom. Gather family members to act out the problems (in addition to your child). If you don't have enough actors for all the parts, use pictures or toys (e.g., dolls). You can choose to solve one problem a day or complete all of them at one time. In addition to using the problems listed here, help your child create his or her own money-sharing problems to act out.

For further insights on helping your child learn the value of sharing money via charity and gifts, see the section, Additional Ideas for Parents, page 191. See also the Letter to the Parents, page 236.

Money-Sharing Problems

Problem Number 1
If I gave Sam four pennies to hold for me and gave Jose three pennies to hold, how many pennies are Sam and Jose holding?

Problem Number 2
Sarah found some pennies and kept six pennies and gave Ezra four pennies. How many pennies did Sarah find?

Problem Number 3
Carmen had four pennies. If I gave her ten more pennies, how many pennies would Carmen have?

Problem Number 4
If I gave everyone at your table two pennies, how many pennies are there?

Problem Number 5
I gave Will five pennies. His friend, Jill had three pennies. Who had more? How many more?

Problem Number 6
Jenny had ten pennies. She gave eight pennies to Billy. How many did she have left?

Problem Number 7
If I had ten pennies and wanted to share them between Max and Pete, how many will each of them get?

Problem Number 8
Isabella had four pennies and Graciela had five pennies. How many did they have all together?

Problem Number 9
If everyone in the class had one penny, how many pennies would there be altogether?

Problem Number 10
If I gave everyone in class today two pennies, how many pennies is that?

Chapter 6
Should We Spend, Save, or Share?

Formative Assessment

In Lesson 6.3, *Benny's Pennies*, students had an opportunity to count pennies. Use this activity as an informal assessment to know who needs further assessing. Look for students who always clear their ten-frames without using the previous number. Watch if those students who clear their ten-frames use one-to-one correspondence (small quantities are being used so students may use one-to-one correspondence without using information about numbers to build the next number). This information generally is not for grading purposes. Use this information to help decide if a child needs further experiences in counting or if further testing is needed.

Students involved in Lesson 6.5, *Using Quarters for Landmarks*, can be observed as they work independently. Use that lesson as an introduction, but follow up with observations using Reproducible 6, capturing information about students' ability to count on from quarters. As you chart, you will be able to decide which students to watch or pull aside for a quick individual assessment.

Formative Assessment Checklist
Chapter 6 Lessons, Should We Spend, Save, or Share?

Student Name	Counts Quarters to a Dollar	Counts On from Quarters with Pennies	Counts On from Quarters with Nickels	Counts On from Quarters with Dimes

Additional Idea$ for Parent$

Helping Your Child Be Financially Savvy with Sharing Money

Young children believe the world is centered on them. The younger our children are, the more likely they are to be self-centered. As they mature their world expands and they begin to notice the needs of others. If we want our children to grow up to be generous and charitable, we should give them opportunities to learn about generosity and charity at an early age.

One of the ways we can help our children is by giving them opportunities to see us being generous and charitable with our money. We need to model generosity. The next time you collect items for donation, include your child in the process. Explain where you are taking the items and why donations are helpful for people in need. Don't hide the good things you do for others!

Help your child participate in giving gifts for holidays and birthdays. Give your child the opportunity to deliver gifts to friends and relatives. This will help her or him experience the joy of giving at an early age. Even prekindergarteners are old enough to shop with you for special gifts; though keep in mind that at that age, the information about the gift probably won't be a secret for long!

CHAPTER 7

Where Do We Keep Our Money?

Understand Banks and Their Various Purposes—From Providing Interest on Savings to Loans and Credit Cards

Overview

The banking industry is very complex. Young children see banks as a place where their parents get money, without understanding that money coming from a bank belongs to the saver or is a loan from the bank. The book *If You Made a Million* is used as a rich source of economic ideas throughout this chapter's lessons, from providing the context for understanding what a bank is to figuring interest on savings and interest on loans.

Lesson 7.1 helps students answer the question "What is a bank?," broadening their understanding of a bank from piggy banks to a financial institution. Students also revisit the concept of goods and services, connecting the financial concept of a bank to services. **Lesson 7.2** gives students an opportunity to work with stacks of coins. In **Lesson 7.3** students are introduced to interest. **Lessons 7.4** and **7.5** introduce students to the concept of loans; in **Lesson 7.5**, the book *One Hen: How One Small Loan Made a Big Difference* allows students to bump into the idea that someone can borrow a small amount of money and eventually be successful enough to change his family, his community, and his country. The lesson reinforces the importance of financial responsibility, personal initiatives, global awareness, giving back, and sharing (a continued theme from Chapter 6). In the final two lessons, students take their understanding of loans one step further, exploring the concept of credit-card loans and gift debit cards.

The Lessons

Formative Assessment
226

Formative Assessment Checklist
227

Literature Used in This Chapter

If You Made a Million by David M. Schwartz

One Hen: How One Small Loan Made a Big Difference by Katie Smith Milway

Don't Forget the Final Project!

This chapter prepares students for the final project, in which they apply the financial savvy they've gained through the lessons in Chapters 1–7 to a real-life financial endeavor. After completing the lessons in Chapter 7, see the final project in the Appendix, page 239–244.

Additional Idea$ for Parent$

Helping your child be financially savvy with saving and borrowing money — 228

What Is a Bank?

An economics lesson introducing the various meanings of *bank*, the concept of *bank* as a financial institution, and its purpose for young learners

Overview

The word *bank* has many meanings. To alleviate potential confusion, the first part of this lesson explores the various meanings of the word, ultimately narrowing in on the financial meaning. Students then engage in a game of coin riddles—reinforcing the concept of a bank as a place to keep money. This is likely the meaning that students are most familiar with, assuming they have or have encountered piggy banks and other means of keeping money safe in their home. Students are then introduced to the story *If You Made a Million*, bringing students closer to understanding a *bank* as a financial institution. Upon a second reading of the book, students revisit the concept of goods and services, connecting the financial concept of a bank to services.

Mathematics Goals

Students will:
- ▶ count by fives, tens, and twenty-fives
- ▶ relate counting to adding five cents to each dollar
- ▶ solve problems involving addition
- ▶ write problems involving money
- ▶ solve problems involving money

Common Core State Standards for Mathematics:

Number and Operations in Base Ten   1.NBT.1
- *Extend the counting sequence*

Operations and Algebraic Thinking   1.OA.5
- *Add and subtract within 20*

Operations and Algebraic Thinking   2.OA.1
- *Represent and solve problems involving addition and subtraction*

Measurement and Data   2.MD.8
- *Work with time and money*

Economics Goals

Students will show:
- ▶ understanding of the Concept of Money by:
  - • recognizing various forms of U.S. currency
- ▶ understanding of the Concept of Goods and Services by:
  - • identifying examples of goods and services
- ▶ understanding of the Concept of Economic Institutions by:
  - • recognizing that there are institutions, such as banks and credit unions

Time

1 class period

Literature Connections

If You Made a Million by David M. Schwartz

Materials

1 small jar wrapped in paper to hide contents and containing 4 dimes and 2 pennies

paper and pencil for each student

small jars wrapped in paper to hide contents, 1 per pair of students

sets of coins, 1 per pair of students (sets should contain no more than 6 pennies, 6 nickels, and 6 dimes each)

My Coin Riddle Recording Sheet (Reproducible 7.1), 1 copy per pair of students

Teaching Directions

Part 1: Understanding the Word *Bank*

1. Gather students in the whole-group area of your classroom. Introduce the word *bank* to them. Explain that bank can mean many things. Define bank in several ways before talking about the definition of bank in financial terms.

2. Tell students that the word *bank* means many things, but the bank they are going to talk about isn't one of those above. Ask students, "Does anyone own a bank?" Give students time to talk about the type of banks they own. (Expect descriptions of piggy banks and other places students put their money.)

Exploring Various Meanings of the Word *Bank*

Ask if anyone has ever fished from a river bank. What do students think the word *bank* means when it is used this way?

Tell students you heard someone say that they could bank on Henry to do his job. What do students think the word *bank* means when it is used this way? (This use of bank is the same as saying you depend on Henry to do his job.)

If you live where it snows, students will be aware of snow banks on the side of the road. What do students think the word *bank* means when it is used this way?

Ask a student to pretend to be an airplane flying around the room (usually young children will spread their arms and tilt as they go around a corner). Explain that when an airplane turns, it tilts so one wing is lower than the other. Pilots would say that they need to bank, or tilt, the airplane when they turn.

Part 2: Exploring the Concept of *Bank* as a Place to Keep Money

3. Hold up a small jar that contains four dimes and two pennies. The jar should be wrapped in paper so that its contents cannot be seen. Tell students that the jar represents a bank. The bank has coins in it. You would like students to ask you questions that will help them guess which coins are in the bank. Answer questions such as "Are these United States coins?" Don't answer questions that will give too much information (such as "How much money do you have in your bank?")

4. After students have asked a few questions, tell them that you are going to give them some clues, one at a time. These clues form a "coin riddle." Students need to think and do a little math in order to figure out what coins are in the bank.

Start with the clue "There are six coins." Ask students, "What could the largest amount be in the bank?" (six dollars). Then ask, "What could the smallest amount be in the bank?" (six cents).

A Coin Riddle (The Clues)

1. There are six coins.
2. There are only two kinds of coins in my bank.
3. There are only dimes and pennies.
4. There is more of one type of coin than the other.
5. There are more dimes than pennies.
6. There are four dimes.

5. Give the second clue, "There are only two kinds of coins in my bank." Explore several possibilities, such as dollars and pennies, nickels and dimes . . . and so on.

6. Give the third clue, "There are only dimes and pennies." Ask students to work with a partner and find all the possibilities if there are six coins and some of them are dimes and some of them are pennies. Make sure students have pencil and paper. When students are finished working with their partners, reconvene as a whole group. Ask students to tell you the possibilities they came up with; create a list for everyone to see.

7. Give the fourth clue, "There is more of one type of coin than the other." Go back to the list and have students help eliminate possible combinations (for example, "three dimes and three pennies" would be eliminated).

8. Reveal the fifth clue, "There are more dimes than pennies." Eliminate other possibilities on the list. This should leave "five dimes and one penny" and "four dimes and two pennies."

9. Read the last clue. Students should eliminate "five dimes and one penny" and know that "four dimes and two pennies" are in your jar.

10. Open your jar (your "bank") and count your coins. Make sure students can verify the coins from your bank.

Part 3: Writing Your Own Coin Riddles

11. Explain that students are now going to have an opportunity to write their own coin riddles. Have students work in partners. Give each pair a small jar that is wrapped in paper so the contents don't show. Ask students to label their jars by writing their names on the paper that covers their jar's contents.

12. Tell students that there are a few coin riddle rules. They need to keep the number of coins to more than three and less than seven (limit the types of coins if you know your students don't have enough experience counting quarters). They should not use more than three kinds of coins.

Coin Riddle Rules

Your jar must contain . . .
• three, four, five, or six coins
• only one, two, or three kinds of coins

13. Give each pair of students a set of coins (see Materials list). Ask students to select coins from their set and put them in their jars. Remember the coin riddle rules! Students may want to put books up around their workspace so no one can see the coins they are putting in their jars. They should cover their sets of coins so the coins in the jar aren't guessed by looking for what is missing from the set.

14. Once students have selected the coins for their jars, they need to work with their partner to write a riddle (clues). Give each pair of students a copy of *My Coin Riddle* (Reproducible 7.1). Circulate, noting any challenges and providing support as needed.

**Teaching Insight:
Sets of Coins**
Put each set of coins in plastic sandwich bags ahead of time. Include a note in each bag that lists the number of coins that should be in it. Have students count the coins against the list before returning each bag to you at the end of the lesson.

Part 4: Editing the Coin Riddles

15. After students have finished writing their coin riddles, have them hand in both their jars and their riddles. Check the riddles to see if they make sense. If there are just a few riddles that don't make sense, take time to meet with those partners to help edit the riddles. If many of the students wrote riddles that don't work, call volunteers from an upper grade or parent volunteers to help students think through their riddles.

Part 5: Sharing the Coin Riddles

16. After the coin riddles have been edited, share a few riddles every day until everyone has had a chance to present their riddles to the class.

Part 6: Understanding *Bank* as a Financial Institution

17. Tell students that they are now going to learn yet another meaning of the word *bank*. Ask students if they've ever visited a bank. Explain that the banks they've described and worked with to complete their coin riddles are similar to the bank they've visited; however, there is one big difference. When you put money in a bank at home, the amount stays the same. If you put a dollar in your bank, when you take it out there will still be a dollar. When you put your money in a bank—a financial institution—the kind of bank in which you can open an account, after some time when you take it out, there is a little *more* money because the banks pay interest (you'll talk about interest later). Banks, credit unions, and savings and loans are all places where people take their money to keep it safe. A bank also provides a way for people to pay bills and buy things without having to carry lots of money.

Part 7: Introducing and Reading the Book

18. Show the book *If You Made a Million* to students. Ask students, "What do you think the book is about?" You will probably get responses that the book is about a million dollars. Confirm that this book is about money.

19. Read *If You Made a Million* to students, making sure they can see the illustrations.

Part 8: Understanding a Bank as a Service

20. Read the book a second time, revisiting the concept of goods versus services (originally introduced in Chapter 5). On the first page, in small print, there is a sign reading, "Feed the fish. Earn 1 cent." This is used to introduce one penny. When you read it, stop and ask your students, "Would feeding the fish be a *good* or a *service*?" Have students explain why they know it is a service. (Feeding the fish is something that is being done for money and is therefore a service.)

21. At the bottom of the same page there is a sign on which Perry is offering pebbles for one cent. Ask your students, "Is Perry selling a *good* or a *service*?" Have students explain why they know that selling a pebble is a *good* and not a *service*. (A pebble is something that is being sold for money and is therefore a product.)

22. Each sign with a job introduces a new coin. Stop at each job and ask students if the sign is offering a good or a service.

23. Reconnect students with their understanding of *bank* as a financial institution. Point out that a bank provides a service; banks and credit unions are organizations that take in deposits, pay interest, make loans, and process checks. The government has many rules for banks and credit unions and makes sure they are safe places for us to keep our money.

**Teaching Insight:
About the Book**
The book is an ALA Notable Book and a School Library Journal Best Book of the Year; its delightful, humorous story seems to cover everything under the money sun—from concepts of interest and bank loans to checking accounts, income tax, and even financing a mortgage.

**Teaching Insight:
How Banks Are Different
from Piggy Banks**
In the back of the book *If You Made a Million* the author includes additional notes aimed at adults; the author gives a good explanation about banks and how they are different from piggy banks. Revisit this with students as necessary.

**Teaching Insight:
Counting Coins**
In addition to exploring goods and services as you read the book a second time, encourage students to practice counting. In the book, with each coin there is a display of ways to make the same value using different coins. Use this as an opportunity to count by fives, tens, and twenty-fives with your students. Take note of the different ways each number is shown in coins and ask students, "Can you think of any additional ways the author didn't include?" (For nickels there aren't any other ways, but if students substitute pennies for nickels they will find other ways for coins worth more than nickels.) Since students have had other opportunities to do this, just quickly listen to a suggestion or two without recording.

Extensions

To further explore students' understanding of a bank, considering doing a data collection activity using the following questions:

- Have you ever been with someone when they drive up to a bank window? (If you have "yes" responses, ask students if they received a treat from the bank. Many banks give treats—such as lollipops—to children at the drive-up window.)
- Have you ever been inside a bank?

Model this after any data collection lesson in this resource, such as Lesson 6.2.

Ideas for Parents

You can use this lesson at home with your child just as it is written here; you will need to be your child's discussion and activity partner. Share your child's coin riddles with friends and family. Read the book in this lesson at home with your child. Encourage discussions in answer to the question "What is a bank?" Instead of doing the data collection extension mentioned at the end of the lesson, think of this as an opportunity for you to visit your bank with your child, whether it be going through the drive-through or actually going inside.

For further insights on making saving and payment transactions a financial learning opportunity for your child, see the section, Additional Ideas for Parents, page 228. See also the Letter to the Parents, page 237.

Reproducible 7.1

My Coin Riddle
Recording Sheet

Names _____

Put your names on your jar.

Coin Riddle Rules

Your jar must contain:

- *Use three, four, five, or six coins*
- *Use only one, two, or three kinds of coins*

Write your riddle:

_____

_____

_____

_____

How Many Coins Are in That Stack?

A lesson in stacking and counting coins for young learners

Overview

As part of the effort to efficiently handle and count money, banks stack and distribute coins in rolls. In this lesson students revisit the book *If You Made a Million* (this book is originally introduced in Lesson 7.1) as the context for thinking about the value of stacks of coins. Students, in pairs, first estimate how many of each coin—pennies, nickels, dimes, and quarters—would be needed to form stacks of coins 1-inch tall. They then convene as a whole group to compare their estimates and make note of possible connections (does the thickness of a coin have anything to do with the number that it might take to make a 1-inch stack?). Students are then given rulers and, back in partners, they measure and count 1-inch stacks, plus determine the monetary value of each. As an extension to this lesson, bring actual rolls of coins into the classroom to study and explore.

Common Core State Standards for Mathematics:

Counting and Cardinality   K.CC.5
  • *Count to tell the number of objects*

Number and Operations in Base Ten   2.NBT.2
  • *Understand place value*

Measurement and Data 2.MD.8
  • *Work with time and money*

Mathematics Goals

Students will:
  ▶ count to tell how many coins
  ▶ skip count by five and tens
  ▶ solve problems involving money

Economics Goals

Students will show:
  ▶ understanding of the Concept of Money by:
    • recognizing various forms of U.S. currency

Materials

Measuring 1-Inch Stacks of Coins Recording Sheet (Reproducible 7.2), 1 copy per pair of students

rulers, 1 per pair of students

a set of coins (20 pennies, 16 nickels, 22 dimes, and 17 quarters), 1 per pair of students

Time

1 class period

Literature Connections

If You Made a Million by David M. Schwartz

Teaching Directions

Part 1: Connecting to Literature

1. Gather students in the whole-group area of your classroom. Revisit the book *If You Made a Million*. Read to the place where the author describes earning a million dollars by taming an ogre. The author says it would take a stack of pennies ninety-five miles high to equal a million dollars. Point out to students that we can't reasonably check a stack of a million dollars' worth of pennies but we are able to think about the worth of pennies in 1-inch stacks—let's try it!

Teaching Insight:
Sets of Coins
Put each set of coins in plastic sandwich bags ahead of time. Include a note in each bag that lists the number of coins that should be in it. Have students count the coins against the list before returning each bag to you at the end of the lesson.

Part 2: Estimating (Recording Sheet Part A)

2. Have students work in pairs. Give each pair of students a set of coins (see Materials list) and a copy of *Measuring 1-Inch Stacks of Coins* (Reproducible 7.2). Ask students to look at Part A: Estimates on their recording sheets. Ask students, "How many of each coin do you think it will take to build a stack of coins one inch tall?" Emphasize that in this part students must estimate (students will get rulers later). Circulate and make note of any challenges as students compare the relative heights of their coin stacks and record their estimates on their recording sheets.

3. After students have recorded their estimates, reconvene as a whole group. Ask students what their estimates are, coin by coin. Listen and record their estimates where everyone can see them. Separate each coin's estimates in the list.

4. When you are finished listing the estimates, ask students what they notice. Look at the estimates and see if there is any connection to the width of a coin and the number they believe will be in a 1-inch stack. Have students compare nickels and quarters. Ask, "What do you notice?" They should notice that nickels are slightly thicker than quarters. It might be difficult for young students to think about thicker coins making a stack where fewer coins are used to reach an inch.

Teaching Insight:
Rulers
In Step 5, you will give students rulers. For the rulers you use, make sure each ruler's measurements start exactly at the end of the ruler and not after a small space before the actual inch measurement begins.

Part 3: Measuring and Counting (Recording Sheet Part B)

5. Give each pair of students a ruler and a set of coins (see Materials list). Ask students to complete Part B: Measuring and Counting on their recording sheets.

   Your students may find one more or one less coin to fill the 1-inch. This is not a problem. The work of counting the number of coins and then counting the value of the coins is more important than the measurement task itself.

6. When students have finished measuring and counting, make sure they have also determined the value of the stacks of coins.

Part 4: Processing the Experience

7. Bring students together to discuss what they found. Because of classroom tools, measurements may vary a little. There may be a difference of one coin in some stacks. If that occurs, create and measure a stack of coins with your whole class. Ask students to think about the size of coins and the number of coins in an inch. You should expect students to describe stacks with thicker coins to have fewer coins in an inch than thinner coins, such as dimes.

8. Explain to students that when coins are purchased in quantities from a bank, usually they are purchased in a roll. Anyone can purchase rolls of each of the U.S. coins. Since coins are different thicknesses, there are different numbers of coins in each. Consider sharing a copy of the following table, which shows the number of coins in a roll and the cost to purchase a roll of coins.

Teaching Insight: The Measurements

Measurements are always somewhat inaccurate depending on the tools we use and the quality of coins. In Part B of the recording sheet, when I measured I found that:

- Eighteen pennies were approximately 1-inch tall. Those pennies are worth eighteen cents.
- Fourteen nickels were approximately 1-inch tall. Fourteen nickels are worth seventy cents.
- Twenty dimes were approximately 1-inch tall. Twenty dimes are worth two dollars.
- Fifteen quarters were approximately 1-inch tall. Fifteen quarters are worth three dollars and seventy-five cents.

Teaching Insight: Differentiating for Younger Students

If you are doing this stacking lesson with children who don't count by fives and tens yet, do Step 5 as a whole group. Use only pennies, nickels, and dimes. Review coin values and then count by ones, fives, or tens to find the value of the coins.

Coins	Number of Coins in a Roll	Cost to Purchase a Roll of Coins
Penny	50	50 cents
Nickel	40	$2.00
Dime	50	$5.00
Quarter	40	$10.00

Extensions

Bring actual rolls of coins to the classroom. Start with a roll of pennies. Cover the information on the roll that indicates the roll's value and the number of pennies. Ask students to think about the 1-inch stack of coins and estimate how many pennies might be in the roll. Uncover the information on the roll and verify the amount of pennies and the value of the roll. Continue with nickels, dimes, and quarters. You may need to actually count the coins in the roll for students to believe how many coins are in a roll. Take time to talk with students about their estimates. Ask, "Did measuring and counting one inch of coins help you estimate the number of coins in a roll? What did you need to know to be able to figure out how much a roll of dimes would cost?"

Idea$ for Parent$

You can use this lesson at home with your child just as it is written here; you will need to be your child's discussion and activity partner. If you are in a store and a clerk opens a new roll of coins to make change, be sure to point out the use of the roll to your child. Explain that businesses buy coins in rolls to use for making change because rolls are easier to keep track of than loose change.

For further insights on making saving and payment transactions a financial learning opportunity for your child, see the section, Additional Ideas for Parents, page 228. See also the Letter to the Parents, page 237.

Measuring 1-Inch Stacks of Coins
Recording Sheet

Names _____

A. Estimates

> *Write how many of each coin you think there will be in a 1-inch stack.*

How many **pennies** in a 1-inch stack?   _____

How many **nickels** in a 1-inch stack?   _____

How many **dimes** in a 1-inch stack?   _____

How many **quarters** in a 1-inch stack?   _____

B. Measuring and Counting

> *Stack, measure, count, and record how many coins are in each stack. Use coin values and write how much the 1-inch stack of coins is worth.*

There were _____ **pennies** in my 1-inch stack.

Those **pennies** are worth _____

There were _____ **nickels** in my 1-inch stack.

Those **nickels** are worth _____

There were _____ **dimes** in my 1-inch stack.

Those **dimes** are worth _____

There were _____ **quarters** in my 1-inch stack.

Those **quarters** are worth _____

What Is Interest?

A lesson introducing the concept of interest and exploring the receiving of interest on savings for young learners

Overview

In this lesson students revisit the book *If You Made a Million* (this book is originally introduced in Lesson 7.1) as the context for thinking about earning interest on money deposited in a bank. Through a problem-solving activity, students pretend to deposit money in a bank and earn interest over a year. Students then convene as a whole group to process their experience and discuss the various ways they may have solved the problem. This lesson is best used with second graders and some first graders. For younger students, consider acting out the problem before having them solve it.

Mathematics Goals

Students will:
- ▶ relate counting to adding five cents to each dollar
- ▶ solve problems involving addition
- ▶ solve problems involving money

Common Core State Standards for Mathematics:

Operations and Algebraic Thinking   1.OA.5
- *Add and subtract within 20*

Number and Operations in Base Ten   1.NBT.1
- *Extend the counting sequence*

Operations and Algebraic Thinking   2.OA.1
- *Represent and solve problems involving addition and subtraction*

Measurement and Data 2.MD.8
- *Work with time and money*

Economics Goals

Students will show:
- ▶ understanding of the Concept of Economic Institutions by:
  - • recognizing that there are institutions, such as banks and credit unions
  - • identifying what it means to save money in an institution

Literature Connections

If You Made a Million by David M. Schwartz

Materials

Solving Problems Involving Interest on Savings Recording Sheet (Reproducible 7.3), 1 copy per student

Time

1 class period

Teaching Directions

Part 1: Introducing and Exploring the Concept of Interest

1. Gather students in the whole-group area of your classroom. Revisit the book *If You Made a Million*. At this point students should be familiar with the book and excited to follow along (it was read in both Lessons 7.1 and 7.2). Read the book again. Eventually you'll reach the part of the book in which, instead of suggestions for spending, the author suggests saving the dollar. The author explains that if you put the dollar in the bank at the end of the year, it will be worth $1.05. The extra five cents is called interest. Stop reading after you read "If you leave it there for fifty years, your ten dollars will grow to $138.02."

2. Introduce and explain the concept of "interest" to students.

Teaching Insight:
Introducing Interest
In the back of the book *If You Made a Million* the author includes additional notes aimed at adults; the author gives a good explanation about banks and how they are different from piggy banks. He suggests that if students are not able to understand fractions, decimals, and percentages, they should skip the next note about interest and compound interest. Children in preK through second grade are likely not ready to work with compound interest. They are, however, able to think about adding a coin to every dollar.

Financial Facts: Receiving Interest

When we go to the bank to make a deposit, the bank takes our dollars. The bank wants to use our money so it is willing to pay something if we leave our money there. The bank makes a promise to pay something extra in addition to the beginning dollars if we leave it for a while—maybe even a year or more. If we go back to the bank, maybe a year later, when we take our money out of the bank, the bank will pay a little more than the original amount we deposited. For example, if we put a dollar in the bank for a year, we might get a dollar plus a nickel when we withdraw our money from the bank. The extra money is called interest.

Part 2: Solving Problems Involving Interest

3. Tell students you need them to help you solve a problem involving interest. Introduce the problem and questions on *Solving Problems Involving Interest on Savings* (Reproducible 7.3), an excerpt from the problem follows.

Pretend that you have twelve dollars. You put twelve dollars in the bank. For each dollar, you will earn five cents each year.

- How much interest will you get from your twelve dollars at the end of the year?
- If you take your twelve dollars and the interest out of the bank at the end of the year, how much money will you withdraw from the bank?

Teaching Insight:
Differentiating for Younger Students

Present the problem in Step 3 to some first-grade students and most second-grade students. With younger students, have dollar bills and nickels available and act out the situation. Ask one student to play the part of a bank customer, giving the banker twelve dollars. Ask another student to play the part of the banker. Tell students to pretend a year has passed. The same student goes back to the banker. The banker gives twelve dollars and places a nickel on each dollar bill. Count the original twelve dollars plus interest.

4. Have students work at their desks or tables. Give each student a copy of *Solving Problems Involving Interest on Savings* (Reproducible 7.3). Explain that they need to solve the problem and record how they did it. Their recording sheets should include pictures, words, and numbers. Circulate as students are working, observing and making notes of any challenges and successes.

Part 3: Processing the Experience

5. When students have finished solving the problem, reconvene as a whole group and give them the opportunity to talk about the way they solved this problem. Discuss students' various strategies. Listen to students; ask the key questions.

Key Questions

What do you know about interest?

How much interest will you earn if you add five cents to every dollar?

How much will you have all together when you withdraw savings and interest?

How did you figure it out?

Ideas for Parents

You can use this lesson at home with your child just as it is written here; you will need to be your child's discussion and activity partner. Follow the specific directions for younger and more experienced students. If your child is not ready to record on the worksheet, act out the problem instead.

For further insights on making saving and payment transactions a financial learning opportunity for your child, see the section, Additional Ideas for Parents, page 228. See also the Letter to the Parents, page 237.

Solving Problems Involving Interest on Savings
Recording Sheet

Name _____

Use pictures, words, and equations to solve this problem. Show your work below.

The Problem

Pretend that you have twelve dollars. You put twelve dollars in the bank. For each dollar, you will earn five cents each year.

How much interest will you get from your twelve dollars at the end of the year?

If you take your twelve dollars and the interest out of the bank at the end of the year, how much money will you withdraw from the bank?

What Is a Loan?

A lesson in understanding the giving and receiving of loans for young learners

Overview

In this lesson students revisit the purposes of a bank, specifically focusing on the question "What is a loan?" and identifying what it means to borrow money from an institution. The book *If You Made a Million* (first introduced in Lesson 7.1) once again provides an invaluable context for helping students understand banking concepts. Once they have an understanding of the meaning of a loan, students solve a problem involving a loan for twelve dollars. Students revisit the concept of interest (introduced in Lesson 7.3) and figure out the total amount they would need to pay the bank back, including interest. Students then convene as a whole group to process their experience and discuss the various ways they may have solved the problem. This lesson is best used with second graders and some first graders. For younger students, consider acting out the problem before having them solve it.

Mathematics Goals

Students will:
- ▶ count dollars and dimes
- ▶ relate counting to adding ten cents to each dollar
- ▶ solve problems involving addition
- ▶ solve problems involving money

Economics Goals

Students will show:
- ▶ understanding of the Concept of Economic Institutions by:
  - • recognizing that there are institutions, such as banks and credit unions
  - • identifying what it means to borrow money from an institution

Common Core State Standards for Mathematics:

Operations and Algebraic Thinking 1.OA.5
- *Add and subtract within 20*

Number and Operations in Base Ten 1.NBT.1
- *Extend the counting sequence*

Operations and Algebraic Thinking 2.OA.1
- *Represent and solve problems involving addition and subtraction*

Measurement and Data 2.MD.8
- *Work with time and money*

Literature Connections

If You Made a Million by David M. Schwartz

Time

1 class period

Materials

Solving Problems Involving Loans Recording Sheet (Reproducible 7.4), 1 copy per student

Teaching Directions

Part 1: Introducing the Concept of a Loan

1. Gather students in the whole-group area of your classroom. Revisit the purposes of a bank—make a list of reasons why we have banks (providing a safe place to keep money, taking in deposits, paying interest, making loans, processing checks, etc.). Ask students, "What is a loan?" Explain that when people need to borrow money, they can go to the bank and ask a banker for money.

2. Revisit the book *If You Made a Million*. Turn to the page where it says "Magnificent! You've earned $50,000. And you've just read about a well-worn, unloved, but perfectly fixable castle for sale. The price: $100,000." This page describes what happens when you want to buy something that costs more than you have. Read the next two pages about paying the bank back month after month. In the back of the book in the "A Note from the Author" section, the author writes about loans and why banks charge interest. Read this section to your students. Further discuss and clarify their understanding of giving and receiving loans.

Financial Facts: Giving and Receiving Loans

The bank takes our dollar and other people's dollars and makes loans to people who have a good idea and need money for a business or who need money to buy a house. When people borrow money from the bank for a business or a house, they have a schedule for paying the money back. The people who borrow money will pay a little interest to the bank on the money they borrowed. For example, for every dollar someone gets from the bank, they will give the bank a dollar back plus a nickel or a dime or some pennies. These loans usually have something that people promise to give to the bank if they don't pay the bank. If people have borrowed money for a house, they usually promise to give the house to the bank if they don't pay. If people borrow money for a business, they usually have something such as a building or a factory they promise to give to the bank if they don't pay. When farmers have a loan on their farm, they agree to give their farm to the bank if they don't pay.

Part 2: Solving Problems Involving Loans

3. Introduce the problem and questions on the *Solving Problems Involving Loans* recording sheet (Reproducible 7.4), an excerpt from the problem follows.

Pretend you had a loan from the bank. Pretend you borrowed twelve dollars and agreed to pay the bank an extra dime for every dollar you borrowed at the end of the year.

- How much interest will you pay in a year?
- What is the total amount you would pay the bank when you paid the twelve-dollar loan plus interest?

Teaching Insight:
Differentiating for Younger Students
Step 3 is best used with second graders and some first graders. For younger students, act out this situation. Ask one student to play the part of the person asking the bank for a loan. Ask another student to play the part of the banker. The banker gives the customer twelve dollars. When the customer returns the twelve dollars, a dime is added for each dollar. Count the amount of money including interest.

4. Have students work at their desks or tables. Give each student a copy of the recording sheet (Reproducible 7.4). Explain that they need to solve the problem and record how they did it. Their recording sheets should include pictures, words, and numbers. Circulate as students are working, observing and making notes of any challenges and successes.

Part 3: Processing the Experience

5. When students have finished solving the problem, reconvene as a whole group and give them the opportunity to talk about the way they solved this problem. Discuss students' various strategies. Listen to students; ask the key questions. Listen to children who may have experienced losing a home or a business to a bank.

Key Questions

How much will you pay back to the bank if you borrow twelve dollars?

How much interest will you pay?

How did you figure it out?

Did anyone think of another way to solve this problem?

How is interest on a loan different from interest on your savings?

Ideas for Parents

You can use this lesson at home with your child just as it is written here; you will need to be your child's discussion and activity partner. If your child is not ready to record on the worksheet, act out the problem instead. Emphasize that whenever you borrow money you have to pay it back, plus a little extra money.

For further insights on making saving and payment transactions a financial learning opportunity for your child, see the section, Additional Ideas for Parents, page 228. See also the Letter to the Parents, page 237.

Reproducible 7.4

Solving Problems Involving Loans
Recording Sheet

Name: _____

Use pictures, words, and equations to solve this problem. Show your work below.

The Problem

Pretend you had a loan from the bank. Pretend you borrowed twelve dollars and agreed to pay the bank an extra dime for every dollar you borrowed at the end of the year.

How much interest will you pay in a year?

What is the total amount you would pay the bank when you paid the twelve-dollar loan plus interest?

How One Small Loan Made a Big Difference

An economics lesson addressing the power of microfinance and introducing the concepts of banking, loaning, and borrowing money for young learners

Overview

The book, *One Hen: How One Small Loan Made a Big Difference* along with its incredibly enriching website, provides a friendly, real-life path for introducing the power of microfinance—economic concepts of banking, loaning, and borrowing money—in addition to reinforcing the importance of financial responsibility, personal initiatives, global awareness, giving back, and sharing (a continued theme from Chapter 6).

The story *My Rows and Piles of Coins* (Lesson 5.5) makes a great companion piece to *One Hen*.

Mathematics Goals

Students will:
- ▶ count to one hundred
- ▶ count within one thousand
- ▶ look for patterns in a group of numbers
- ▶ count by hundreds
- ▶ solve problems involving money

Common Core State Standards for Mathematics:

Counting and Cardinality   K.CC.1
  • *Know number names and the count sequence*

Operations and Algebraic Thinking   2.OA.1
  • *Represent and solve problems involving addition and subtraction*

Number and Operations in Base Ten   2.NBT.2.8
  • *Understand place value*
  • *Use place value understanding and properties of operations to add and subtract*

Measurement and Data   2.MD.8
  • *Work with time and money*

Economics Goals

Students will show:
- ▶ understanding of the Concept of Earning Money by:
  - • discussing that work provides income to purchase goods and services
- ▶ understanding of the Concept of Wants and Needs by:
  - • identifying basic human needs
- ▶ understanding of the Concept of Economic Institutions by:
  - • recognizing that there are institutions, such as banks and credit unions
  - • identifying what it means to borrow money from an institution

Literature Connections

One Hen: How One Small Loan Made a Big Difference by Katie Smith Milway

Materials

chart paper or some means of displaying a T-chart for students to see

paper and pencil for each student

Time

1 class period

Teaching Directions

Part 1: Introducing and Reading the Book

1. Gather students in the whole-group area of your classroom. Show your students the front cover of the book *One Hen: How One Small Loan Made a Big Difference*. Tell students that the boy's name is Kojo. Kojo lives in Ghana. Locate Ghana on a map or a globe with students. Ask students what they think Kojo's needs might be. Expect students to name some of the things talked about in earlier chapters, such as food, clothing, and shelter. Explain that Kojo and his mother are having difficulties getting these needs because Kojo's father died.

2. Read *One Hen: How One Small Loan Made a Big Difference* to students, making sure they can see the illustrations.

Part 2: Discussing the Book

3. When you are finished reading, discuss the story and economics concepts with students. Ask key questions such as those shown below, referring to the book to support the answers.

Teaching Insight: About the Book

One Hen: How One Small Loan Made a Big Difference is the inspiring true account of Kojo, a boy who lives in Ghana, Africa. Families in his village pool their savings into a community bank that makes loans available to members. Kojo borrows a small amount of money to buy a hen. He sells extra eggs at the market and saves his money to buy more hens, eventually building the largest poultry farm enterprise in West Africa. Kojo's story illustrates how one person, with a good idea, gets a loan and eventually changes his life, his community, and his country. Today the real Kojo, Kwabena Darko, sits on the board of Opportunity International, a global microfinance nonprofit organization.

Key Questions

What is a loan? Where did Kojo get his loan?

Did Kojo make a good decision when he spent his money? Why was it a good decision?

Would the story have ended the same if Kojo had bought candy with his money? How would he have repaid the loan if he had bought candy?

What did Kojo's chicken need to survive and lay eggs? (Use this as an opportunity to reinforce needs such as food, water, and shelter.)

What did Kojo do to provide shelter for his hen?

What did Kojo do to feed his hen?

Where did Kojo sell his eggs? Were the eggs a good or a service?

Eventually Kojo had twenty-five chickens and could sell more eggs. How did he spend his money then?

How did Kojo change his community? (Talk about the people he hired and the people who opened shops to sell things to his employees.)

Kojo paid taxes. What did the government do with that money?

Part 3: Introducing the Concept of Microfinance

4. In the back of this book there is a section about helping families like Kojo's. This section tells us that if we donate ten dollars to a microfinance program, that ten dollars could help more than a hundred families. Sometimes it is hard for children to understand the magnitude of ten dollars helping one hundred people. Explain that in their final project (see the corresponding Appendix, page 239) they are going to get an opportunity to make a difference in some people's lives; the final project will involve them in microfinance—helping poor people.

5. Tell students that there are organizations that make loans to people internationally. There are also organizations that help people here in the United States. Get students thinking about places to donate in their community or in one of the international locations. Habitat for Humanity is one place that makes microfinance part of their efforts. Most communities have a local food bank that assists families through hard times.

Financial Facts: Microfinancing

Microfinance is the lending of money to the poor. Sometimes this is done by charitable organizations. Sometimes the money is lent by a group of people who pool what little money they have but are able to loan money as a group. Often, when poor people need money they borrow from informal moneylenders who are not regulated like banks. Sometimes these loans are made with very high interest rates. Often these loans are made to women with children because such women are apt to stay near their homes and therefore will be easy to track down for collection purposes. One small loan in this system that doesn't use traditional banking can make a difference in many lives.

Part 4: Exploring Microfinance Loans Using a T-Chart

6. Create a T-chart similar to the T-chart shown here. Explain that you want to record how many people would be helped for each ten-dollar contribution. Start by making a T and labeling the left side *Each $10 loan*. Label the right side *Number of people helped*.

Each $10 loan	Number of people helped
1	100
2	200
3	300
4	
5	
.	
.	
.	
10	

Teaching Insight:
Using a T-chart
T-charts are a graphic organizer used by mathematicians to examine facets of a topic. If your students have not worked with a T-chart before, be sure to set this up with a simpler problem first. One possible example would be to use a T-chart to show the number of children (in the column on the left) and the corresponding number of eyes (in the column on the right). Second-grade students and many first-grade students will be able to complete their own T-charts using the pattern of the numbers for four and five ten-dollar donations. Many students will extend the pattern or notice that when there are 2 ten-dollar bills, the number of people helped is two hundred; when there are 3 ten-dollar bills, the number of people helped is three hundred.

Teaching Insight:
Visualizing One Hundred People
Younger children might have difficulties visualizing one hundred people; if so, consider doing this activity: count out one hundred 3-by-3-inch sticky notes. Pass them out to students so each student has an even number of sticky notes. Ask students to draw one face on each sticky note. Give the first students finished an additional sticky note until all one hundred sticky notes have faces drawn on them. Arrange the sticky notes in a 10-by-10-inch array. Count the faces with students. Be sure to count the faces by ones and then by tens. Show students a ten-dollar bill. Tell students that, according to the author of the book *One Hen: How One Small Loan Made a Big Difference*, one ten-dollar donation can help one hundred people. Ask students, if there were 2 ten-dollar donations, how many people could be helped? Continue asking for three or more if students are ready to handle bigger numbers.

7. Give each student a plain sheet of paper. Do the first 3 ten-dollar loans together.

8. Ask students to now complete their own T-charts. Direct them to continue their T-chart to include 4, 5, and 10 ten-dollar donations. While students are working, circulate, observing and making notes of any challenges and successes.

Part 5: Processing the Experience

9. When students have completed their T-charts, reconvene as a whole group and ask key questions.

Key Questions

How did you know how many people were helped when there were 4 ten-dollar loans?

How did you figure out how many people were helped when there were 10 ten-dollar loans?

You weren't required to figure it out, but how many people were helped if there were 7 ten-dollar loans?

Extensions

For more information about the project described in the book and further teaching ideas, access the website for *One Hen: How One Small Loan Made a Big Difference*—www.onehen.org.

Idea$ for Parent$

You can use this lesson at home with your child just as it is written here; you will need to be your child's discussion and activity partner. Read the book in this lesson at home with your child. Encourage discussions about giving back and sharing money. Do the activities on the book's website with your child.

For further insights on making saving and payment transactions a financial learning opportunity for your child, see the section, Additional Ideas for Parents, page 228. See also the Letter to the Parents, page 237.

Should I Use a Credit Card?

A lesson introducing credit cards and the subsequent interest

Overview

At this point in the chapter students should have a sound understanding of what a bank is and some of its purposes—specifically providing a safe place to save money, paying interest, and making loans. In this lesson students take their understanding of loans one step further, exploring the concept of credit-card loans. Students revisit the concept of interest (introduced in Lesson 7.3) and figure out the total amount they would need to pay the bank back, including interest, if they were to purchase an item using a credit card. Students then convene as a whole group to process their experience and discuss the various ways they may have solved the problem. This lesson is best used with second graders and some first graders. For younger students, consider acting out the problem before having them solve it.

Common Core State Standards for Mathematics:

Operations and Algebraic Thinking   1.OA.5
 • *Add and subtract within 20*

Number and Operations in Base Ten   1.NBT.1
 • *Extend the counting sequence*

Operations and Algebraic Thinking   2.OA.1
 • *Represent and solve problems involving addition and subtraction*

Measurement and Data   2.MD.8
 • *Work with time and money*

Mathematics Goals

Students will:
 ▶ extend the counting sequence
 ▶ relate counting to adding ten cents to each dollar
 ▶ solve problems involving addition
 ▶ solve problems involving money

Economics Goals

Students will show:
 ▶ understanding of the Concept of Economic Institutions by:
  • recognizing that there are institutions, such as banks and credit unions
  • identifying what it means to borrow money from an institution

Time

1 class period

Materials

a copy of the current logo for MasterCard and the current logo for Visa (reference current MasterCard/Visa websites)

Solving Problems Involving Credit Cards Recording Sheet (Reproducible 7.6), 1 copy per student

Teaching Directions

Part 1: Introducing the Concept of Credit Cards

1. Gather students in the whole-group area of your classroom. Ask students, "Have you ever seen a credit card?" Show students a copy of MasterCard and Visa logos. Most students have watched their parents or other adults make purchases with credit cards. Ask students what they know about credit cards. Listen to their ideas about credit cards. Let students know that sometimes you use credit cards because they are convenient ways to pay for things, such as the gasoline you put in your car.

2. Carefully explain what happens when a credit card is used. Make connections to the knowledge students have gained in previous lessons about loans (borrowing money) and interest.

Financial Facts: Credit-Card Loans

When we use credit cards, we are borrowing from the bank. Like loans learned about in previous lessons, a bank may put a limit on the amount of money one can borrow using a credit card. However, credit-card loans do not entail something we have promised to give the bank if we don't pay the money back.

The bank likely charges more interest when they loan money with credit cards. When we use a credit card, we expect a bill. If we do not pay the bill in full the month it is received, the bank will charge interest on the remaining amount until it is paid.

Part 2: Solving Problems Involving Credit Cards

3. Explain to students that if you borrow a dollar from the bank using a credit card, you might have to pay as much as twenty-five cents interest for every dollar you spend. Introduce the problem and questions on the sheet *Solving Problems Involving Credit Cards* (Reproducible 7.6), for example:

Teaching Insight:
Using a Quarter for Interest Rates
Using a quarter for each dollar is not a true reflection of interest rates. Quarters are landmark amounts for students. The addition of a quarter is used for the mathematics, not the accuracy of interest rates.

> Pretend you used a credit card to buy a toy for twelve dollars. Your bank will charge you twenty-five cents in interest for every dollar you spend with your credit card.
> - How much interest will there be on this twelve-dollar credit-card loan?
> - How much will you pay altogether when you pay the twelve dollars plus interest?

Teaching Insight:
Differentiating for Younger Students
This lesson is best used with second graders and some first graders. For younger students, act out this situation. Ask one student to play the part of the person using a credit card to make a purchase. Have another student play the part of a clerk in a store. The first student buys something that costs twelve dollars. To pay, that student gives a credit card to the store clerk. The student playing the part of the store clerk pretends to swipe the credit card in the machine and then gives a receipt for the item purchased. Stop the action at this point. Explain that the first student bought something that cost twelve dollars. After the bank processes the credit-card information, a bill will be sent that adds twenty-five cents for every dollar spent. Use dollars or paper that represent twelve dollars. Put one quarter on each of the dollars. Count to make sure you have twelve dollars and twelve quarters. Tell students you want to know how many dollars there are in all. Group the quarters in stacks of four. Explain that four quarters are worth one dollar. Count the twelve dollars and then continue to count the stacks of quarters. You should discover that there are three dollars in interest and a fifteen-dollar cost in all.

4. Have students work at their desks or tables. Give each student a copy of *Solving Problems Involving Credit Cards* (Reproducible 7.6). Explain that they need to solve the problem and record how they did it. Their recording sheets should include pictures, words, and numbers. Circulate as students are working, observing and making notes of any challenges and successes.

Part 3: Processing the Experience

5. When students have finished solving the problem, reconvene as a whole group and give them the opportunity to talk about the way they solved this problem. Discuss students' various strategies. Listen to students; ask key questions such as those shown here.

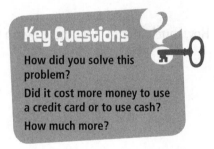

Key Questions

How did you solve this problem?

Did it cost more money to use a credit card or to use cash?

How much more?

Idea$ for Parent$

You can use this lesson at home with your child just as it is written here; you will need to be your child's discussion and activity partner. If your child is not ready to record on the worksheet, act out the problem instead. Emphasize the convenience of using credit cards for purchases such as buying fuel for your car; however, also explain that if you pay the balance due on the card sooner, you will pay less interest.

For further insights on making saving and payment transactions a financial learning opportunity for your child, see the section, Additional Ideas for Parents, page 228. See also the Letter to the Parents, page 237.

Solving Problems Involving Credit Cards
Recording Sheet

Name _____

Use pictures, words, and equations to solve this problem. Show your work below.

The Problem

Pretend you used a credit card to buy a toy for twelve dollars. Your bank will charge you twenty-five cents in interest for each dollar you spend with your credit card.

How much interest will there be on this twelve-dollar credit-card loan?

How much will you pay altogether when you pay the twelve dollars plus interest?

Using Debit and Gift Cards

A data collection lesson introducing debit and gift cards for young learners

Overview

This lesson follows Lesson 7.6; once students have an understanding of credit cards, they should also understand that there are debit and gift cards—which look like credit cards, but do not carry the same implications. Students have the opportunity to connect their personal experiences to the lesson, answering and collecting data on the question "Have you ever received a gift card for a special occasion?" Students solve a problem in which a gift card is used in a purchasing transaction. The problem helps students further understand and clarify the important difference (interest!) between a debit or gift card and a credit card.

Mathematics Goals

Students will:
- ▶ count the responses in data collection categories
- ▶ represent and interpret data

Common Core State Standards for Mathematics:

Number and Operations in Base Ten   K.MD.3
- *Classify objects and count the number of objects in each category*

Measurement and Data 1.MD.4
- *Represent and interpret data*

Measurement and Data 2.MD.10
- *Represent and interpret data*

Time

1 class period

Materials

an example of a birthday greeting card

an example of a gift debit card

sticky notes, 1 per student

chart paper or some means of displaying written lists for students to see

Teaching Directions

Part 1: Introducing the Concept of Debit and Gift Cards

1. Gather students in the whole-group area of your classroom. Show them a birthday card and explain that it is something you receive on your birthday. Ask, "Has anyone ever received a birthday card?" Many students will raise their hands "yes!" If you have someone in your class who recently had a birthday, let that child briefly share the experience.

2. Now show students a gift debit card. Explain that we may call birthday cards and gift debit cards "gift cards" though they are very different. In addition, tell students that although the gift debit card may look like a credit card, it is not. Tell students your card has twenty dollars on it for you to spend. Explain that this is a set amount of money already given to you on the gift debit card; when you use the card, unlike a credit card, you will not get a statement asking that you pay for the charges. You also don't pay any interest on the money that you spend using the gift debit card. Emphasize that a gift debit card is just like cash; if you lose it, it is just like losing money.

3. Ask students, "Have you ever received a gift card for a special occasion?" Listen while students share their experiences. Students may want to tell what they spent their gift cards on.

Part 2: Collecting Data

4. Create a two-column chart where everyone can see it. Title the chart, "Have you ever received a gift card for a special occasion?" Label one column *Yes* and one column *No*.

5. Give each student a sticky note. Ask them to write *Yes* or *No* on their sticky note, according to their answer to the question.

6. Have each student come up to the chart and place his or her sticky note in the appropriate column.

Part 3: Discussing the Data

7. Discuss the data on the chart and then ask key questions like those shown here.

Key Questions

What do you notice when you look at our chart?

Which group had the most?

Which group had the least?

Part 4: Problem Solving

8. Present the following problem to students:

> Let's pretend you found a toy that costs twelve dollars. You are using a debit gift card that your aunt gave you. No interest is charged on the money you spend with this card. How much are you paying for the toy in all?

Give students a little time to think about this. Listen as students explain their thinking. Some students may be confused and still want to add coins to each dollar. Some students may think you are asking a trick question since nothing is added to the twelve dollars.

9. Discuss the fact that the toy cost stays at twelve dollars because this is not a loan. Compare the cost to the twelve-dollar toy bought with a credit card (Lesson 7.6).

Idea$ for Parent$

With a few modifications, you can successfully use this lesson at home with your child. For the data collection part, have your child survey friends and family members. Discuss the data with your child. Make sure your child understands the costs associated with using a gift debit card. Remember, even young children can think about the cost of something purchased with a gift card instead of a credit card!

For further insights on making saving and payment transactions a financial learning opportunity for your child, see the section, Additional Ideas for Parents, page 228. See also the Letter to the Parents, page 237.

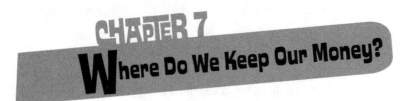

Formative Assessment

- Can students explain basic human needs?
- Can students explain if these needs are the same or different than the needs of Kojo's hen (Lesson 7.5)? (Food, shelter, and water are needed for all animals including people.)
- Are students able to explain the difference between goods and services?
- Were students able to understand the interest problems?
- Were students able to explain how they solved the interest problems?
- Were students efficient in their drawings or did they use too much detail in their problem-solving pictures?
- Were students engaged in these activities?

When working with young children, you will notice that sometimes children with rote counting skills to one hundred fail to use one-to-one correspondence when counting objects. Often these same students randomly point and say counting words without tagging each object with only one counting word. These students need more experiences counting and need opportunities to watch their peers counting with one-to-one correspondence and tagging. It is sometimes useful to know who tags and uses one-to-one correspondence, so you can match students who need help with students who model good counting skills. Use the *Formative Assessment Checklist* (Reproducible 7) to help keep track of those students who need more experiences counting, as well as for planning future instruction.

- Were students engaged in number writing? (If not, consider varying the type of writing instrument or adding grips to pencils.)
- Were students less likely to reverse numbers when number samples were available?
- Were students able to understand the last number said was the quantity of pennies?

Formative Assessment Checklist
Chapter 7 Lessons, Where Do We Keep Our Money?

Student Name	Rote Counts to ____	Uses One-to-One Correspondence	Tags Each Penny with the Number Name

CHAPTER 7

Where Do We Keep Our Money?

Additional Idea$ for Parent$

Helping Your Child Be Financially Savvy with Saving and Borrowing Money

There are two big ideas introduced in this chapter. The first is about saving money and having an opportunity to earn interest on money when we deposit it in a banking institution. The second idea is that when we borrow money, we have to pay it back with interest.

Children learn what we model for them. There is no need for your child to know how much money you have saved or how much money you owe on your house or business or credit cards. However, when you put money in savings, help your child to be aware that you save money. It is important for children to know you are saving for something—whether it be for their college education, a rainy day, or your retirement. Saving just to be saving money might not make sense to a child.

You can also make your child aware of when you make regular payments on loans or credit cards; explain to her or him that your payment also includes interest since you are using the bank's money. Let your child know that whenever you borrow money through a bank loan or a credit card, you pay a little extra (called interest) for using money you don't have.

Lastly, include your child in visits to your bank, whether it be via the drive through or actually going inside.

Appendix

Letters to the Parents

Economics Objectives

Each lesson's economic goals align to the following economics objectives. See page xix for more information on the creation of these objectives.

By the end of second grade, students will show:

1. Understanding of the Concept of Money by:
   a. recognizing various forms of U.S. currency
   b. recognizing that different countries have different coins
   c. identifying that people use money to purchase goods and services

2. Understanding of the Concept of Earning Money by:
   a. discussing different types of jobs that people do
   b. discussing the requirements of various jobs
   c. discussing that people make goods and perform services
   d. discussing that work provides income to purchase goods and services
   e. identifying jobs in the home, school, and community

3. Understanding of the Concept of Goods and Services by:
   a. identifying examples of goods and services
   b. identifying goods that people make
   c. identifying services that people provide
   d. explaining the difference in purchasing and bartering for goods and services
   e. identifying that people are buyers and sellers of goods and services
   f. discussing that people save money for future goods and services

4. Understanding of the Concept of Wants and Needs by:
   a. identifying basic human needs
   b. explaining how basic human needs can be met
   c. describing the needs of a family
   d. explaining that individuals and families cannot have everything they want
   e. identifying examples of wanting more than we have
   f. explaining why wanting more than we have requires people to make choices
   g. explaining some of the consequences of unplanned spending

5. Understanding of the Concept of Economic Institutions by:
   a. recognizing that there are institutions, such as banks and credit unions
   b. identifying what it means to borrow money from an institution
   c. identifying what it means to save money in an institution

Letter to the Parents

Chapter 1: What Is Money?

Dear Parents,

We will soon begin Chapter 1 of *Why Can't I Have Everything? Teaching Today's Children to Be Financially and Mathematically Savvy, Grades PreK–2.* The lessons in this resource will help us meet both our mathematics and our economics standards.

During this first chapter, titled "What Is Money?", students will identify and trade coins. This chapter lays a foundation for knowing the coins and their values, counting combinations of coins, and eventually counting change back from a purchase.

It is important for coin identification that real coins are used. I am asking each child to provide 10 dimes, 20 nickels, and 50 pennies to use during this school year. If you would like this $2.50 returned to you, please send me a letter requesting return of the coins at the end of the year. Any coins not returned will be used to purchase end-of-year snacks for students and be used next year to introduce coins to students in the next class.

Some lessons use socks as containers for holding coins. I am asking for donations of single socks (without holes) to use with coin-counting lessons.

At home, reinforce what has been introduced at school by letting your child see, touch, and handle coins from your pocket or purse at the end of the day. Identify coins as your child handles them.

Letter to the Parents

Chapter 2: Where Do We Get Our Money?

Dear Parents,

We will soon begin Chapter 2 of *Why Can't I Have Everything? Teaching Today's Children to Be Financially and Mathematically Savvy, Grades PreK–2*.

In Chapter 2, titled "Where Do We Get Our Money?", we look at how we get money. This includes discussions about gifts, allowances, and money received from the tooth fairy.

If you haven't begun to give your child an allowance, you might consider it. If you are planning to start paying your child an allowance, consider the following questions:

How much money should I give? How should I pay? When should I pay? How often should I pay? Should this allowance be linked to jobs around the house? Do I give an allowance to older and younger siblings? Do I pay the same amount or do older children receive more? What do I want to teach my child about managing this money?

As you pay an allowance, you may want to consider paying with a different denomination of coin each time. Pay with quarters. The next time, pay in all dimes. Pay with a check. Pay with two kinds of coins. Each time, help your child count the money.

Letter to the Parents

Chapter 3: Do We Have Enough Money?

Dear Parents,

We will soon begin Chapter 3 of *Why Can't I Have Everything? Teaching Today's Children to Be Financially and Mathematically Savvy, Grades PreK–2.* The idea of giving and receiving change is introduced and used in money-related problem solving.

The title of this chapter is "Do We Have Enough Money?" When children watch parents, often they think adults can buy anything they want. They really don't see the ways we determine our budgets and decide if we have enough money to buy what we want.

If we want to help our children learn to consider if they have enough money to buy what they want, we have to avoid saying "you can't afford that" and start saying, "Let's count your money and see if you have enough to pay for it." Sometimes when children are confronted with the problem of not being able to buy something because it is too expensive, they will choose a less expensive alternative. Consider this a learning experience. As adults, when we can't afford what we really want, we often choose a less expensive alternative. What a great thing to teach our children!

Letter to the Parents

Chapter 4: Why Can't We Have Everything?

Dear Parents,

We will soon begin Chapter 4 of *Why Can't I Have Everything? Teaching Today's Children to Be Financially and Mathematically Savvy, Grades PreK–2*. The economic ideas explored in this chapter are wants and needs. We will continue to think of why we can't have everything and think about the consequences of spending without thinking.

At home, reinforce the lesson that once money is spent, it is really gone. It is easy to rescue our children when they spend their allowance and have no money for something they really want. When we give children money after they spend foolishly, we are teaching them to hurry and spend, without thinking and planning, because someone will help them out if something important comes along. Find a way for your child to earn extra money if there is something really important to buy after the allowance is gone. Payment for extra chores is a great way to fill the gap.

Don't control what your child buys with an allowance. Try to guide by asking questions such as "Is that something you really need? Is there something better you are saving money to buy? Is there something you would rather have?" Encourage delayed gratification. Encourage price comparison.

If your child still wants to make foolish purchases, just consider it a learning experience and let your child buy what he or she wants.

Letter to the Parents

Chapter 5: How Do We Earn Money?

Dear Parents,

We will soon begin Chapter 5 of *Why Can't I Have Everything? Teaching Today's Children to Be Financially and Mathematically Savvy, Grades PreK–2*. This chapter is titled "How Do We Earn Money?" It explores sources of money beyond allowances and tooth fairies.

The literature used in this chapter, *Arthur's Funny Money*, introduces the idea of making money. Arthur uses a good idea, makes a sign, invests his savings, and sets up business. After Chapter 7, I will ask students to do something similar. Keep that in mind and help your child start thinking about a service (such as teaching someone to dance or braid hair) or a good they could sell at our school during a one-day market (such as an old toy or homemade cookies). More details will follow as we get closer to the end of this unit.

One of the best ways for children learn about the value of money is to earn money. Your child is too young to go door-to-door selling products or asking for jobs, but payment for chores well done at home will help your child develop a sense of how hard it is to make a dollar. Children should not be paid for every task they do at home—just special jobs that allow them to earn some money.

For our final project, every child will not only need to bring a way to earn money but also need to have earned about a dollar at home to spend at our market.

Letter to the Parents

Chapter 6: Should We Spend, Save, or Share?

Dear Parents,

We will soon begin Chapter 6 of *Why Can't I Have Everything? Teaching Today's Children to Be Financially and Mathematically Savvy, Grades PreK–2*. This chapter is titled "Should We Spend, Save, or Share?"

It is natural for children in prekindergarten through second grade to be a little self-centered. Their world expands as they mature and they begin to notice the needs of others. In our world today it is ever more important to teach children not only the consequences of unplanned spending and the benefits of saving but also the value of sharing. One of the ways we can help our children is by giving them opportunities to see us being generous with our money and being charitable. Also, children learn about the joy of giving by participating in gift giving for holidays and birthdays. Young children can help you shop for gifts. They will enjoy delivering gifts to friends and relatives.

For our final project we will be donating some or all of the proceeds to a charity. _____ and _____ are two charities I am considering. Both of these charities fulfill basic needs of people who live in our community. Please let me know if you have other ideas where the class should donate money after our final project.

Letter to the Parents

Chapter 7: Where Do We Keep Our Money?

Dear Parents,

We will soon begin Chapter 7 of *Why Can't I Have Everything? Teaching Today's Children to Be Financially and Mathematically Savvy, Grades PreK–2*. This final chapter is all about where we keep our money.

The banking industry is complex. Young children see banks as a place where their parents get money. Children don't always understand where that money came from. In our world today it is important to teach children the consequences and rewards of borrowing money and to convey the idea that when you borrow money you have to return it with a little bit of extra money. In this chapter children explore the idea of interest on savings and loans, and the differences in debit and gift cards and credit cards.

Our final project will take place on _____. Each child needs to have one way to make money. This can be by performing a service. An example of that might be teaching someone how to do something. Another way to make money is by selling a good. An example of that could be selling a toy that is no longer used or bringing a food item to sell. We will make posters at school advertising what we are selling and how much it costs. Each child also needs to bring up to one dollar to spend at our market. We will be giving about ____ % of our earnings to our charity.

We are always looking for volunteers to help children count money and make change. Please let me know if you are able to be there.

Letter to the Parents

Final Project

Dear Parents,

We have finished the lessons in *Why Can't I Have Everything? Teaching Today's Children to Be Financially and Mathematically Savvy, Grades PreK–2*. We are preparing for our final project.

On _____ we will have a Market Day where all students will be both buyers and sellers. Each student needs to have a service to sell or a product to sell. Your child will have brainstormed possibilities of ways to make money but if you have a better idea, please plan with your child and help complete the attached business plan. Please return the business plan as soon as possible.

I will be giving each child $____ in change. This is a return of part of the money you donated for classroom use. Your child may bring up to $_____ in additional funds to spend at the market. I am asking that all goods or services sell for less than $_____. Please help your child price what is being sold.

We will have a donation jar for coins children decide to donate to a charity. We have chosen _____ as our classroom charity. Please talk to your child about a possible contribution when you work on the business plan. No child will be forced to donate to a charity.

I am looking for volunteers to help with our market. You would need to be in our classroom by _____ o'clock. Any help would be appreciated.

Market Day

Overview

The lessons in Chapters 1 through 7 have provided students with diverse opportunities to become both financially and mathematically savvy. In this final project, children create a market in the classroom—providing a unique opportunity for students to tie together their financial and mathematical ideas into one setting, from further understanding the value of money to earning it, pricing and selling a good or service, and giving and receiving change. Each student must decide on a service or a good to sell in order to make money. Students use a business plan to outline their strategy for earning money. They advertise what they are selling and supervise their own stall, setting prices, taking money, and making change. Following the market's close is a discussion of goods and services, setting prices, scarcity, and giving to charity.

Mathematics Goals

Students will:
- ▶ count coins to determine how much money there is
- ▶ use place value to count coins
- ▶ work with equal groups to gain a foundation for multiplication
- ▶ solve problems involving money

Economics Goals

Students will show:
- ▶ understanding of the Concept of Money by:
  - •recognizing various forms of U.S. currency
  - •identifying that people use money to purchase goods and services
- ▶ understanding of the Concept of Earning Money by:
  - •discussing that people make goods and perform services
- ▶ understanding of the Concept of Goods and Services by:
  - •identifying examples of goods and services
  - •identifying goods that people make
  - •identifying services that people provide

Common Core Standards for Mathematics:

Counting and Cardinality   K.CC.1.4.a.b.c.5.7
- *Know number names and the count sequence*
- *Count to tell the number of objects*
- *Compare numbers*

Number and Operations in Base Ten   1.NBT.1.2.a.b.c
- *Extend the counting sequence*
- *Understand place value*

Operations and Algebraic Thinking   2.OA.4
- *Work with equal groups of objects to gain foundations for multiplication*

Number and Operations in Base Ten   2.NBT.1.a.b.2.3
- *Understand place value*

Measurement and Data   2.MD.8
- *Work with time and money*

Materials

chart paper or some means of displaying written
  lists for students to see

paper for posters (butcher paper or large
  construction paper)

$1.00 in change for each student

white construction paper, 1 sheet per student

index cards, 1 per student

Business Plan (Reproducible A.1), 1 per student

After Market Day (Reproducible A.2), 1 per student

Letter to the Parents, 1 per student

Time

Part 1: 30 minutes
Part 2: 1 class period
Part 3: 1 class period

**Teaching Insight:
Differentiating the Sets of
Coins**

Each student will need one dollar
in coins for Market Day. For very
young students, you may want to
limit the sets of coins to pennies
and dimes. You may also want to
reduce the amount in each set to
fifty cents.

Teaching Directions

Part 1: Preparing for Market Day

1. Gather students and tell them they will be having a Market Day in their classroom to earn money. Refer to literature you have already used: *One Hen: How
   One Small Loan Made a Big Difference* (Lesson 7.5), *Ox-Cart Man* (Lesson 5.4),
   and/or *My Rows and Piles of Coins* (Lesson 5.5). All three of these books refer
   to a market. Make sure your students understand that a market is a place where
   people come together to buy and sell goods and services. Explain that they will
   be figuring out a way to make money by selling
   either a good or a service.

2. Refer back to *Arthur's Funny Money* (Lesson 5.1).
   Ask if anyone remembers the service Author did to
   earn money. Help students to think of services they
   could perform during Market Day to earn money.
   Suggestions to get them started could include teaching friends to dance, braiding hair, and/or polishing
   fingernails. List the ideas where everyone can see
   them.

3. Next refer back to *Ox-Cart Man* (Lesson 5.4) and
   talk about the things the man and his family made
   to sell at market. Brainstorm with students and make
   a list of goods they could sell on Market Day. Suggestions to get them started could include gently used
   toys, homemade cookies, and/or store-bought candy
   that is bought in quantity and sold individually.

**Teaching Insight:
Inviting Other Classes**

If yours is the only class in your
school doing a Market Day, you
may want to invite other classes to
shop at your market. Have students
work in groups to make posters
advertising Market Day. Then
visit other classes and invite the
students to shop at your market.
Shopping time might be during
recess or a prearranged time in
class. The amount of time needed
for Market Day will vary depending
on the number of classes/students
participating. Note that very young
students will need more assistance
on Market Day; for these students
you may want to limit the market
to your class only.

4. Choose a charity for donations from market proceeds. Habitat for Humanity and your local food bank both provide help within most communities. Add other charities that interest you or your class. This is also an opportunity to review basic needs and wants with students.

5. Explain to students that there are various other preparations that need to be completed prior to Market Day. Use the list below to guide everyone through the completion of each preparation.

Preparations for Market Day

- ❏ Send the corresponding Letter to the Parents (see page 238) home with each student.
- ❏ Have each student complete a Business Plan (see Reproducible A.1). You will need to send these home for parent assistance.
- ❏ If inviting other classes to Market Day, create posters to advertise the event.
- ❏ Create individual signs to say what is being sold and the cost.
- ❏ Create open/closed signs to use during Market Day.
- ❏ Prepare and label a jar with the charity name(s). This jar will hold student donations.
- ❏ Count coins equaling one dollar into individual plastic sandwich bags for each student in the class.
- ❏ For classes with very young students, ask volunteers to help on Market Day.

Teaching Insight: Creating Signs for Market Day
Consider creating signs the day before Market Day. Ask students if they remember what Arthur did in *Arthur's Funny Money* (Lesson 5.1) when he decided to wash bikes (Arthur's sister gathered materials while Arthur made a sign telling how much he was charging). Give each student a piece of white construction paper and ask them make a sign telling what they are selling and how much they are charging. This is a good time to talk about pricing with students. Tell students they should price what they are selling at a price they would be willing to pay if they were buying. Limit amounts to less than one dollar. If you are working with very young students, give them choices for prices that are multiples of tens (ten cents, twenty cents . . .). Also give each student an index card. On one side they should write "Open" and on the other, "Closed." Tell students there are times when they can close their shops so they can go shopping. (They should put a Closed sign on their desks when they leave.) Decide ahead of time who will leave and when they will leave so all of the market stalls aren't closed at the same time. Give students more than one time to shop.

Part 2: It's Market Day!

6. The day of the market, arrange your classroom so shoppers can move in front of desks to look at what is being sold. Give each student one dollar (or the amount you've decided on) in change.

7. Make sure students have the appropriate signs. Remind students of when their shop is open and closed (when they will be shopping).

8. Announce that Market Day is on. Open your market to only your class or to your invited classes. Circulate and help students as necessary during the opening times of Market Day. Bring volunteers into your classroom for further assistance. Give a warning when the market is going to close.

Part 3: Processing the Experience

9. After Market Day closes, take time to talk with your students. Begin by asking your students to count their money. Give each student a copy of Reproducible A.2, *After Market Day*, and ask him or her to complete it. Assist students who need help counting money. Afterward consider asking the key questions below.

10. When your discussion is over, take a look at your charity jar. Ask students, "Is there anyone who wanted to contribute to our charity but didn't have a chance to contribute?" Give students an opportunity to put money in the charity jar.

11. Explain to your students that they have been entrepreneurs. Write the word *entrepreneur* where everyone can see it.
Tell students that an entrepreneur is someone who has his or her own business and gets all the rewards along with all the risks of the business.

Extensions

Consider using the coins in the charity jar for a final estimating/money-counting project.

Key Questions

How much money did you make?

If you took away the dollar I gave you, how much money did you make?

What sold the best? Why do you think it was such a good seller?

Who sold the most?

Did you sell everything? Could you have sold more if you had more?

What would you do differently if we had another market day?

Did anyone drop her or his price during the market? Why?

Is there anyone who tried to sell the same thing as someone else but with a different price? Which sold first? What was the price?

Business Plan

Student Name _____

I plan to sell _____

_____

_____

(Please plan to individually wrap any food items.)

These are the things I need to bring from home:

_____

_____

I hope to make $ _____

I plan to contribute _____ of my earnings to our class charity.

My parent:

____ is able to volunteer to help at our market.

____ is not able to volunteer to help at our market.

Parent Signature _____

Please return this form by _____

After Market Day

Student Name _____

What was sold? _____

_____

Count your money.

    How many pennies? _____

    How many nickels? _____

    How many dimes? _____

    How many quarters? _____

Total value of all your coins: _____

Literature Used in Each Chapter

The lessons in each chapter of this resource include connections to literature. The literature is invaluable for opening financial discussions with children. Here is a list of the literature organized by the chapter that first introduces it. One of my favorite things to do when getting a resource with literature connections is to take the bibliography directly to my local bookstore and get the books. Here you go.

—*Jane*

Chapter 1: What Is Money?
Adler, David A., *Money Madness*, Holiday House, 2010.
Anderson, Jon Lee, *Smart About Money*, Grosset & Dunlap, 2003.
Hill, Mary, **Welcome Books: Money Matters series** (*Dimes, Dollars, Nickels, Pennies, Quarters*), Children's Press, 2005.
Maestro, Betsy, *The Story of Money*, HarperCollins, 1995.
Williams, Rozanne Lanczak, *The Coin Counting Book*, Charlesbridge Publishing, 2001.
Worth, Bonnie, *One Cent, Two Cents, Old Cent, New Cent*, Random House Books for Young Readers, 2008.

Chapter 2: Where Do We Get Our Money?
Bate, Lucy, *Little Rabbit's Loose Tooth*, Dragonfly Books, 2010.
Berenstain, Stan and Jan, *The Berenstain Bears' Trouble with Money*, Random House Books for Young Readers, 1983.

Chapter 3: Do We Have Enough Money?
Harris, Trudy, *Jenny Found a Penny*, Millbrook Press, 2007.
Holtzman, Caren, *A Quarter from the Tooth Fairy*, Cartwheel, 1995.
Silverstein, Shel, "Smart" in *Where the Sidewalk Ends*, HarperCollins, 1974.

Chapter 4: Why Can't We Have Everything?
Simon, Norma, *All Kinds of Children*, Albert Whitman & Company, 1999.
Torres, Leyla, *Saturday Sancocho*, Farrar, Straus and Giroux, 1999.
Viorst, Judith, *Alexander, Who Used to Be Rich Last Sunday*, Atheneum, 2009.

Chapter 5: How Do We Earn Money?
Hall, Donald, *Ox-Cart Man*, Live Oak Media, 2004.
Hoban, Lillian, *Arthur's Funny Money*, HarperCollins, 1984.
Judge, Lita, *Pennies for Elephants*, Hyperion Book CH, 2009.
Mollel, Tololwa M., *My Rows and Piles of Coins*, Clarion Books, 1999.

Chapter 6: Should We Spend, Save, or Share?
Brisson, Pat, *Benny's Pennies*, Harcourt Children's Books, 1999.
Polacco, Patricia, *Chicken Sunday*, Putnam Juvenile, 1998.
Williams, Vera B., *A Chair for My Mother*, Greenwillow Books, 1984.

Chapter 7: Where Do We Keep Our Money?
Milway, Katie Smith, *One Hen: How One Small Loan Made a Big Difference*, Kids Can Press, Ltd., 2008.
Schwartz, David M., *If You Made a Million*, HarperCollins, 1994.

Additional Literature Connection$

Following is a list of additional recommended literature for helping children be financially and mathematically savvy.

Allen, Nancy Kelly, *Once Upon a Dime: A Math Adventure*, Charlesbridge Publishing, 1999.

This book is a fantasy about a boy who notices a tree growing on his farm. This tree produces different kinds of money, depending on what fertilizer is used. In addition to addressing the figure of speech "money grows on trees" (see Lesson 2.2), this book gives students an opportunity to explore different coins and their values.

Berenstain, Stan and Jan, *The Berenstain Bears' Dollars and Sense*, Random House Books for Young Readers, 2001.

The Berenstain Bears' *Trouble with Money* is first introduced in the lessons in Chapter 2. This second Berenstain Bears book continues the financial fun, leading to discussions of managing money, allowances, and check writing. The book includes a series of tear-out checks (just like they use in Bear Country!) for check-writing practice.

Blood, Charles L., and Link, Martin, *The Goat in the Rug,* Aladdin Paperbacks, 1990.

This gentle, heartwarming book is based on a true story of a weaver and her goat who lived in the Navajo Nation at Window Rock, Arizona. It can be used to further explore the concept of goods and services, explain the production of Navajo rugs (a scarce good), and explore the use of natural resources to produce a rug. It may nicely fit as an extension to the reading of *Ox-Cart Man* (Lesson 5.4).

Lied, Kate, *Potato: A Tale from the Great Depression,* National Geographic, 2002.

Written about the time period when the author was eight years old in Kansas, this is a Great Depression era book describing how one family managed to get the things they needed. Economic ideas that can be connected to this story include goods and services, bartering, and money.

Pilkey, Dav, *The Paperboy,* Scholastic Inc., 1999.

The Paperboy is a Caldecott Honor Book. This beautiful book tells a simple story of a boy and his dog getting up to do a job while the rest of the world still sleeps. It is an ideal companion for conversations around jobs and earning money.

Shaw, Nancy, *Sheep in a Shop,* Sandpiper, 1994.

Sheep in a Shop tells the story, in rhyme, of sheep who want to buy a birthday present for their friend. When they don't have enough money to pay for what they want, they make a swap. The economic idea bumped into with this book is bartering.

Smothers, Ethel Footman, *The Hard-Times Jar,* Farrar, Straus and Giroux, 2003.

The Hard-Times Jar is the story of Emma, the daughter of migrant workers who follow the crops. The family saves money in a jar for "hard times" when they can't earn any money. Economic ideas include the importance of working hard to earn money and the idea of how limited resources affect a family. Another economic idea is the need to produce different goods in different locations, the reason why migrant workers must move from place to place to harvest different crops.

Whelan, Gloria, *Jam & Jelly by Holly & Nellie,* Sleeping Bear Press, 2002.

Holly's family lives in Michigan. Holly needs a coat for next winter or she won't be able to go to school when it is cold and snowy. Holly and her mother search for berries in the forest and make jam and jelly to sell. They set up a stand and sell their goods, saving the money for Holly's new winter coat. Economic ideas include wants and needs and saving money for things that are needed.